Edward Heath

Musick

Musick is an insearchable and excellent Art, which rejoiceth the Spirits and unloadeth Grief from the heart, and consisteth in time and number.

Musick alone with sudden Charms can bind
The wand'ring sense, & calm the troubled mind.

W. Clark Script.

G. Bickham Sculp.

Edward Heath

MUSIC
A Joy for Life

Sidgwick & Jackson London

To my father and mother,
who have made this, and
so much else, possible.

Half-title page: Eighteenth-
century engraving by George
Bickham from *The Musical
Entertainer*
Title pages: Rehearsing the
LSO in the Prelude to *Die Meistersinger*
for their seventieth anniversary
concert, 1974

Designed by Paul Watkins
Picture research by Philippa Lewis

First published in Great Britain in 1976
by Sidgwick and Jackson Limited

Copyright © 1976 by Dumpton Gap
Company and Sidgwick and Jackson
Limited

ISBN 0 283 98349 3

Printed in Great Britain by
The Garden City Press Limited
for Sidgwick and Jackson Limited
1 Tavistock Chambers
Bloomsbury Way, London WC1A 2SG

Author's note

In this book I have tried to express what
music means to me and the part it has played
in my life. I have not set out to write a primer
for those wishing to learn an instrument; nor
to provide a comprehensive coverage of the
entire musical scene. This book merely
describes some of those aspects of music which
I have enjoyed over many years. I hope it
will be sufficient to arouse the interest of
others not yet acquainted with such pleasures.

I have been greatly helped by Virginia
Ashcombe, who has sorted and handled my
programmes, all of which I have kept since I
was fourteen, and by Robert Armstrong who
took part in music-making at 10 Downing
Street and Chequers and who has also read
parts of the manuscript. The latter was typed
by Iris Jollye, Mildred Scott and Ann
Whowall to whom I express my thanks for
their patience, understanding and skill.

E.H.

2 September 1976

Contents

1 Beginning

On holiday in Villefranche, August 1965. My godson,
Lincoln Seligman (left) is playing the guitar. Dominic
Seligman (sitting by me) now plays the organ and piano,
and writes music. He is playing the Grieg Piano Concerto
at Harrow this term (winter 1976). Madron Seligman is
playing the accordion and Roderick Seligman is playing
the trumpet. Roderick played the trumpet in the Harrow
School Orchestra when I conducted it at School Songs

My father used to say to me when I got sick to death of playing scales and arpeggios, particularly on summer evenings when other attractions loomed large in a boy's life: 'Stick to it! Once you've mastered it, nobody can ever take it away from you. Your music will be a joy for life.' At that time this did not seem much of a consolation. It wasn't far to cycle to the beach for a swim, or to the vicarage garden for tennis with the parish youth club – and those grinding scales and arpeggios* became ever more complicated as one got further and further into the finger exercises. Would they never come to an end? One of the lessons I had to learn then applies to so many other things in life as well: the ultimate result depends on a mastery of technique, or rather, the best very often cannot be obtained without that technique. And technique is something which has to be maintained throughout life. In his final judgement my father was absolutely right: as you absorb music, so it becomes part of your life. It can't be taken away from you.

I did not come from a particularly musical family, though we quite frequently had music in the home. Both my father and mother were children of large families, most of whose members still lived in the village of St Peter's-in-Thanet, or in the seaside town of Broadstairs nearby, and they all kept closely in touch. When, on Saturday or Sunday evening, my brother and I went as children to visit them, the grown-ups would often gather round the piano, after some coffee and sandwiches, to sing. It made a break from playing whist or rummy, card games which bored both my brother and me. The songs they sang were Victorian, or at the latest Edwardian, but they still formed the repertoire customary on such occasions in the twenties and thirties. Indeed, as a Member of Parliament, I still hear them sung today, fifty years later, at gatherings where old-age pensioners and other groups are being entertained by local singers who certainly know well the tastes of their listeners.

'Roses of Picardy' and 'Love's Old Sweet Song' were firm favourites. My father, who had a light tenor voice, usually contributed an English version of an aria from Verdi's *Il Trovatore*, '*Ah, che la morte*', commonly rendered as 'Ah! I have sigh'd to rest me'. The meaning of this was not entirely clear to me, but it was a good tune. It has, however, had a long enduring effect which has prevented me from enjoying that work of Verdi's, for whenever we reach the point where Manrico slides into this aria against the background chanting of the '*Miserere*' I find myself once again mentally 'sighing to rest me' and I want to break into hilarious laughter. Almost always the sessions came to an end with Arthur Sullivan's 'The Lost Chord', followed by 'When you come to the end of a perfect day'. These were obviously not works of any great significance but as light music they served their purpose well and the quality of their craftsmanship was high. Not only could they be sung by distinguished vocalists at

'Nobody can ever take it away from you'

* A glossary of musical terms and biographical notes on composers mentioned in this book are given on pages 198–204.

social functions, a mayor's banquet or a society's annual dinner, but the family could also sing and play them in the home and gain satisfaction from them. It was at a time when radio was still in the process of establishing itself and before television had appeared. We had to make our own entertainment, and this was a natural way of doing so. In modern terms it was 'participation', though nobody ever dreamed of calling it that. Only my grandparents sat back in their chairs and listened, sometimes criticizing or occasionally applauding; for the rest of us, to stand round the piano and sing was the thing to do.

The pianist on these occasions was almost always an aunt on my mother's side. She played well and occasionally invited me to her small home in Margate where I sometimes succeeded in getting her to sit down at the piano and play for me. She usually played the popular works of the time, hardly ever those of the classical masters. 'Autumn' by Chaminade produced a lovely melody with the rustling of the leaves in the accompaniment, a rather wintry storm and the final fall of the leaves from the trees. Durand's 'First Valse' – somewhat reminiscent of Chopin's 'Minute Waltz' – was whisked off at a tremendous pace though with a sentimental interlude in the middle. Paderewski's Minuet gave her an opportunity to explain to me how this simple, catchy work had been composed by a man who was not only one of the greatest pianists of his day but had also been Prime Minister of his country.

My favourite, for which I always asked at the end of these personal recitals, was Grieg's 'Wedding day at Troldhaugen'. How beautifully it evokes the atmosphere of the scenes he is depicting; the clip-clop of the ponies' hooves as they draw the sleigh of the bridal couple to the church, a cheerful theme for the occasion building up over them, chords crashing out from one end of the piano to the other as the bells ring out for the arrival of the bride at the church door. Inside all is hushed; we listen to the organ quietly playing through the service. Then the bride and bridegroom are away; more bells, the sound of hooves gradually fading far into the distance until the piece is brought to an end with the usual thunderous chord. That was the one I liked best and I wanted to be able to play it myself. Today it is forgotten, like most of Grieg's music except for the 'Suite from *Peer Gynt*' and the Piano Concerto. It used to be possible to get it on a record by Arthur de Greef, the acknowledged authority at that time on Grieg's Piano Concerto. Now, alas, his recording has disappeared from the catalogue.

Seeing how keen I was and sensing that I might have some talent, my aunt urged my parents to let me learn the piano. The problem was how to get an instrument on which to learn. My parents had only just returned to St Peter's from Crayford, some twenty miles south-east of London, where they had gone to live in the middle of the First World War, six months after I was born,

Nº1 in E♭   Nº2 in F   Nº3 in G.   Nº4 in A♭   Nº5 in A.

SUNG BY

MADAME ANTOINETTE STERLING.

THE LOST CHORD

Song

WITH PIANOFORTE & HARMONIUM (AD LIB) ACCOMPANIMENT

THE WORDS BY

Adelaide A. Proctor

The Music by

ARTHUR SULLIVAN.

Price 2/- net

AL ACCOMPANIMENTS IN THE KEY OF
A PIANOFORTE SOLO BY KUHE, AND FOR

BOOSEY & C°
GENT STREET, L
AND
SEVENTEENTH STREET
BE SUNG IN PUBLIC WITHOUT

THE LOST CHORD (2).

It flooded the crimson twilight,
Like the close of an Angel psalm,
And it lay on my wearied spirit,
With a touch of infinite calm.

Nº1 in B♭   Nº2 in C   Nº3 in D

ROSES OF PICARDY

SONG

WORDS BY

FRED. E. WEATHERLY

MUSIC BY

HAYDN WOOD

Price 2/- Net

CHAPPELL & C° LTD.
50, NEW BOND STREET, LONDON, W.1.
NEW YORK & SYDNEY.
PRINTED IN ENGLAND

Copyright, MCMXVI, by Chappell & C° Ltd.

6758

Edvard Grieg; his was the
first piano concerto I studied

so that my father could work on building aircraft in the Vickers factory there. He was now foreman on a building site for a local contractor. He was renting our house and to buy a piano in these circumstances was no mean undertaking. But both my parents wanted to encourage me and were prepared to make sacrifices to do so. Eventually they decided to commit themselves to buying a new instrument and one Saturday afternoon we set off to the main music shop in Margate, Thornton Bobby, a shop well known in the area for its range of musical equipment. We looked at a variety of pianos and listened to what the salesman had to say about them. Finally, relying very largely on the manager's judgement and advice, my father agreed to buy a piano made specially for Thornton Bobby and sold under their own name. My aunt, who was with us, thought it had a good touch – something in pianos to which I have since learned to attach importance – and also considered that it would wear well. It certainly did, for it remained in our home for forty years. The price was £42, to be paid in twenty-four monthly instalments. It was a good buy and it made an exciting present on my ninth birthday.

The local music teacher was Miss Locke, the daughter of the man who kept the flower shop opposite the parish church. She agreed to teach me and to come to the house once a week throughout the year to give me an hour's lesson. She was insistent, however, that I would have to take it seriously and practise regularly every evening in between her weekly lessons; she relied on my parents to see that this was carried out. Thus began the hours of learning how to finger scales, each hand singly, both hands together, scales of every type and range and sweeping arpeggios covering a scale with three leaps at a time. These were combined with elementary pieces, usually those set for examinations by the musical authorities. As I worked at these basic tasks, Grieg's 'Wedding Day' seemed a long way away. Gradually, however, I began to embark on works which gave me, musically, more satisfaction. I was always in too much of a hurry and became impatient with Miss Locke's insistence that I should get each piece technically absolutely correct before I moved on to another. What I was after was the musical experience, the opportunity to express feeling and emotion in pieces of different kinds, according to my moods. I wasn't always so bothered about making sure that every note came out exactly as it was intended by the composer. I was more intent upon finding an outlet for my own inner fantasies. If there was one gap at this stage in my musical understanding, it was a failure to relate all the work I was doing on scales and other aspects of technique to the pieces I was then starting to play. If I had fully realized then that this was necessary in order to master the works on which even at that time my heart was set, I might have been a little less liable to become enraged by the sheer drudgery of it all.

I was nine when I started to learn the piano; I was forty-nine when I began sailing seriously. It would be difficult to find a more complete contrast in approach to two aspects of my life which have given me such satisfaction. Curiously enough, on one occasion a stranger approached me with a request for me to sign his copy of my book on sailing which he had been given for Christmas, and when I asked him whether he'd enjoyed it, he replied, 'Yes, and as a result I've taken up learning the piano.'

'Reading *Sailing* led you to take up the piano?' I asked somewhat incredulously.

'Yes,' he replied, 'I had always wanted to play the piano but I was too diffident to do anything about it. I thought at my age I would look silly. After I had read your book I said to myself "if he can start sailing at forty-nine, there's no reason why I shouldn't start learning the piano at forty-one." My daughter's eleven and she wanted to as well, so now we learn together. We keep each other up to the mark, though I must say,' he added rather ruefully, 'it is a bit difficult at times to keep up with her.'

I was delighted. Of course he was right. I have known much older people who have begun to learn to play an instrument, often a piano or an electronic organ. If you can do it within the family, so much the better. It is not a question of getting to the point where you can show off to the neighbours, let alone play in public or become a concert pianist. It is a means of self-expression, of understanding more about the music to which you listen, of giving yourself pleasure in your home. For those who are attracted to the organ there is always the possibility of being able to fill an empty organ stool in the local parish church. In many villages today, the vicar or the minister has a problem in finding someone who can play regularly for the services. Such a post also provides an opportunity for training and building up a choir as well as leading congregational singing. I know of few things more worthwhile, both for organist and congregation, than full-throated, though musically understanding, singing in the body of the kirk.

Next door to the fine Norman church of St Peter's-in-Thanet, which dominated the village, was a farm, the barns and farmyard, with cows bellowing, being just by the entrance to the vestry where the choir practised every Friday night. Opposite was the village High Street, on one side the Red Lion, on the other Mr Creasy the pork butcher, who displayed in his window not only sides of his home-fed pigs but also such delicious morsels as pig's chitterlings, liver, brains and trotters. My brother and I were allowed to choose the meal we wanted on our birthdays. Invariably I went for one of these delicacies. We always had round pats of Mr Creasy's sausage meat for breakfast on Sunday mornings as a special treat. They were better value than sausages already in the skins, said my mother.

If the village was dominated by the church from on high, on the ground it was under the all-pervasive influence of Sergeant Fairbeard, who seldom went into the church but was not averse

St Peter's, Thanet, the Norman church in which I was christened and confirmed, where I was a chorister and where I learnt to play the organ

to slipping through the back door of the Red Lion. For us boys he was a force to be watched and contended with. Not for him all the elaborate machinery of the juvenile courts and probation officers, in so far as they existed at that time. His simple but effective approach was to make sure that if you got up to any mischief and were found out your parents quickly got to know all about it and immediately took the necessary action. This was life at St Peter's in the twenties.

At Christmas time in 1934, we gained a distinguished resident in the house next to the farm, the painter Walter Richard Sickert. As I used to cycle past the house to the church I could see his paintings hanging on a clothesline in the garden to dry, gently twirling with the breeze. In particular there was one of Edward VIII, the cause of considerable controversy when it was exhibited at the Leicester Gallery. It was found to have been painted with the aid of photographs, a process which is nowadays fairly common, but which at that time was thought to be so heinous a crime that some critics automatically attacked it.

I only once met Sickert. One wintry evening we opened the gate in the wall of his house Hauteville, went up the gravel garden path and sang two carols outside his door. Neither pressing the bell nor using the knocker elicited any response, but eventually the curtain at the window was drawn aside and through the chink we saw a small, wizened, grey-bearded face. Almost immediately the curtain slipped back again. We waited. Then the door, on a chain, was opened a fraction. 'Go away!' said Sickert, and we left.

I have always had the greatest respect for Sickert as a painter and draughtsman, as well as a writer. One of the first works I bought to hang on my walls when I started collecting after the Second World War was a signed etching of his *Ennui*. I got it for the small sum of £19 from the Leicester Gallery, where that splendid character Oliver Brown, with his instinctive flair for spotting promising contemporary artists, was still presiding.

Our reception by Sickert may not have been wholly out of character, as a story that Sir Alec Martin told me illustrates. Sir Alec, for many years head of Christie's, who had a holiday home at Kingsgate, near Broadstairs, taught me almost all I know about pictorial art. He was a close friend of Sickert's and after his death his executor. He told me how Sickert abandoned his studio in London and came to St Peter's because of the depression of the thirties. A number of people had been trying to help Sickert at this time, including Sir James Dunn, who had commissioned twelve portraits, including those of himself, his wife (later Lady Beaverbrook), Lord Beaverbrook and Lord Castlerosse. Interested in the progress of this venture but not having heard anything about it for some time, Sir James went along to Sickert's London studio, only to find it empty. After some investigation by his staff, he discovered that Sickert had moved to St Peter's; one

day he decided to drive down to see him there. On arrival, he too went through the gate in the wall at Hauteville and up the gravel path. After banging on the door several times, he saw the curtains at the window pulled aside and Sickert's face peering through. 'Come along, Sickert,' said Sir James, 'I want to talk to you about those pictures I commissioned.' The face disappeared and after a further interval the front door was slightly opened. 'How are my pictures going?' Sir James demanded, to which Sickert replied, 'How would you like it if your wife were having a baby and I came banging at your door demanding to know how it was going?' and slammed the door in his face.

I was attending the village church school and, having started to learn the piano at nine, it was natural that I should try to become a chorister at the local parish church. After an audition with the organist Arthur Tatham I was accepted and told that I would be expected to attend the boys' rehearsals on Tuesday evenings, a complete choir rehearsal on Fridays, and Matins and Evensong on Sundays. Once a month I would also be expected to sing at Choral Communion and from time to time there would be special occasions such as weddings and funerals at which the choir would be required. The financial remuneration would be a penny halfpenny for each practice and twopence halfpenny on Sundays – old pence, of course. The total sum would be paid at the end of every three months. I should add that weddings – though not funerals – were sometimes more remunerative, and when the daughter of the local doctor in Broadstairs got married, not only were we paid half a crown each for singing at the service but the whole choir was invited to the reception afterwards. For us, that was an unforgettable occasion.

It was a fact of English musical life that practically every leading composer, conductor, organist or music administrator received his basic grounding in church music. The Salvation Army too has contributed to the training of other musicians, in particular wind instrumentalists; two trumpet-playing contemporaries of mine at grammar school, both of whom learned their instruments in the local Salvation Army band, later went on to become first and second trumpets in the BBC Symphony Orchestra. In the nineteenth century it was the cathedral organists who not only played for the services and trained the choir but also themselves wrote much of the music. In addition, they usually conducted the local choral society which was accompanied either by an amateur orchestra or by one of the provincial orchestras brought in for festival occasions. Most notable of these celebrations, of course, and the oldest established, is the Three Choirs Festival, rotating each year between Worcester, Gloucester and Hereford. Being grounded in church music gave all these musicians a sound basis for a wide variety of activities. Some would say that it put them in a musical straitjacket from which they were never able to break out. Others can point to Edward Elgar and, a generation later,

14

Sir William Walton, who was a chorister at Christ Church, Oxford; he has written a number of short works for church choirs in addition to his masterpiece *Belshazzar's Feast*

William Walton as composers of remarkable individuality who were not bound by their church upbringing, whether Roman Catholic or Anglican.

In the choir in St Peter's-in-Thanet we were brought up on a musical diet which must have been typical of most parish churches fifty years ago. It was a well-balanced choir of some twenty-four boys and twelve men. The organist was a good choir trainer who, at the same time, believed strongly in giving a lead on the organ which would produce bold congregational singing. The anthems on Sunday mornings tended to be of two kinds. On the one hand there were the individual pieces taken from major choral works by Handel, Haydn, Mozart and Mendelssohn; on the other there were anthems typical of the English church composers of the time. Many of these are still sung in our churches and cathedrals. Among the most popular then were 'The Wilderness', 'O Saviour of the World', 'O Taste and See' by Sir John Goss, 'God is a Spirit' by William Sterndale Bennett, 'If the Lord Himself had not been on Our Side' by Dr Thomas Attwood Walmisley, and many others by less well-known composers such as 'Hail Gladdening Light' by George C. Martin. But my particular favourite was and has long remained the anthem by Samuel Sebastian Wesley 'Blessed be the God and Father of our Lord Jesus Christ'. Perhaps it is because in due course I became treble soloist and the middle section of the anthem is a beautifully written treble part, 'Love one another with a pure heart fervently'. In some quarters this work by Wesley is now much disparaged, as I think, unjustifiably; praise for his other major anthems should not be allowed to obscure the balance and the craftsmanship of this work.

At Christmas and Easter we had the opportunity of a change. The carol service on the Sunday evening after Christmas consisted of two or three groups of well-known carols, almost entirely taken from Novello's collection. The *Oxford Carol Book*, with its wide variety of carols from many countries, some of them in splendid harmonizations, had not then made its impact on church choirs. Nor had the form of service on Christmas Eve at King's College, Cambridge, become as widely known as it is today as a result of being broadcast on radio and television. One work was always included so long as we had our splendid baritone soloist Mr Boardman with us. That was *Nazareth*, composed by Charles Gounod. How well he used to develop that flowing, melodic line! 'Though poor be the chamber,' he vibrated. With what emotion did we answer him in the choruses! We choristers were terrified of him. He was a broad-shouldered, well-built man who never disguised his views when he thought the choir was unworthy of his performance. Nor did he ever hesitate to chide us in an attempt to get us to do better.

At Easter we normally performed one major work on the evening of Good Friday. It was for many years Sir John Stainer's

Crucifixion, a simple work less often heard today, but one which when well sung can still be effective. Later we turned to a weightier and more complex work, Gounod's *Redemption*, which proved much more difficult to master. Later still we sang *The Passion according to St Luke* by Bach, much shorter and simpler than either the St Matthew or St John Passion. I have never understood by what authority this work has been attributed to Johann Sebastian Bach but it certainly provided a contrast to both Stainer's *Crucifixion* and Gounod's *Redemption*.

St Peter's-in-Thanet must have been one of the first churches to change over completely to the English Hymnal. Perhaps it was because the vicar at the time, the Reverend C. H. S. Mathews, was a remarkable man who, after spending some of his earlier years in Australia, had returned with the reputation of being a forceful preacher and something of a radical. The English Hymnal gave us the opportunity of appreciating straight away some splendid new hymn tunes, in particular Vaughan Williams's magnificent setting of 'For All the Saints', surely one of the finest ever written. Yet one thing always puzzled me about this, or rather the words to which it was set. Time and again, as a boy, I sang:

> Through gates of pearl streams
> In the countless host

I long wondered what 'pearl streams' were. No one ever bothered to alter our breathing and punctuation in those lines so that the countless host were made to stream in through gates of pearl! A small point, but perhaps it emphasizes how important it is to make sure that singers understand the meaning of the words they are mouthing. Only then can they have any hope of putting real colour, light and shade and spirit into their performance.

The knowledge of church music which I was imbibing at this time was supplemented by the performances of the Broadstairs Choral Society, a local body of some sixty to eighty singers which gave one or two performances a year, with orchestra. While I was still a chorister there was no place for me in such a body but I was usually invited to sell programmes at the concerts. As a result of being at these performances, and the rehearsals for them, I became intrigued by the whole process of conducting. It seemed to me that having control over a choir and orchestra, shaping them to produce the sound one wanted, having soloists singing out of one's hand, so to speak, was really something worthwhile. I was quite soon to become involved.

My voice broke. I moved from the lower to the upper choir stalls and began to sing in a rather limited baritone voice, never quite reaching a tenor register with any ease, nor having the resonance to sink to the depths of a true bass. Nevertheless, I was able to take part in all the choral work we were then doing, as well as to join in singing madrigals and part-songs in groups which used to meet in a few people's homes.

What a pity it is that all too seldom now we gather in each other's homes for this purpose, especially as so much of this music was written by our own composers. Many of those who sang madrigals and part-songs together formed the nucleus of a mixed voice choir which competed regularly in the musical festivals which were a feature of our area. The founder having decided to move to a rather warmer part of the south coast, I was invited to become their conductor. I was now sixteen and welcomed the opportunity to take responsibility for a choir of some thirty sopranos and altos, tenors and basses. We continued to take part in the festivals and, though I was by far the youngest of any of those taking part, we had considerable success. Indeed, although many of the members of the Broadstairs Glee Club, as it was called, had wide experience of this sort of musical activity, they seemed to respond to being led by one so young and to take a pride in it.

After my voice broke, I also started to learn the organ at the parish church. The organ itself was an example of a solid well-balanced instrument, built by Walker, with what is termed a 'tracker action'. This means that the key is pressed down by the weight of the finger without mechanical assistance. The more stops that are out, the heavier the pressure required. As it had three manuals, or keyboards, and each could be coupled, or interconnected, the pressure required when playing with full organ was quite considerable. On the other hand, this form of action required a clean finger technique. Nothing on the keyboard could be smudged. Unless one's finger was pressing down with the full weight required, the note did not speak and the result was plain to everyone listening. The modern pneumatic or electric action is infinitely easier to handle and requires only the lightest of touch; but I doubt whether it insists on precision in the same way as its predecessor.

Once again I had to embark on the hard chores of technical exercises. This time, in addition to the work on the keyboard, there was the introduction of the pedalboard for the feet. There were not only exercises for the left hand alone and the right hand alone, but also for the feet, first separately and then together. Gradually I was working towards a stage where both hands, sometimes on separate manuals, would be co-ordinated with my feet on the pedals. Yet, somehow, practising in this way gave me rather more satisfaction than scales and arpeggios on the piano. What soon became abundantly clear to me was that the technique of playing an organ is in every respect different from that needed for the piano. On the piano, the light and shade, the strength and quality of the sound, depend entirely upon the touch, modified only by the sustaining and dampening pedals. On the organ, the touch itself cannot affect any of these qualities. The touch can provide the rhythm and precision but everything else is produced by the registration on each manual, the combination

of stops used, the coupling of the manuals and the volume of the sound allowed by the opening or closing of the swell boxes.

Our parish organist had a leaning towards the French organ composers, particularly the more brilliant of them, such as Guilmant and Widor, but he started me off, after some simple pieces, with the short Bach preludes and fugues. Then I moved on to Bach's longer works and the Mendelssohn sonatas. Occasionally, I had the opportunity of playing for services. Accompanying the psalms was always the trickiest part and leading the congregation in the hymns the most thrilling; it was, after all, the only occasion on which I could use full organ, though it was indicated to me at times that my choice of registration for both psalms and hymns was thought to be a little too vivid. Psalm 107 provides plenty of opportunity for this in its description of the storm and subsequent calm affecting 'They that go down to the sea in ships'. 'Does the organ at such times give you a sense of power?' I am often asked. 'Yes' is the answer. But not of power over people: it is the power of contributing sound to the general uplift of those making music together.

While I was learning the organ and conducting the mixed voice choir I began to study the more theoretical aspects of music in harmony and counterpoint. I was able to do this under the senior music master, Mr G. C. L. Neville, at my grammar school, Chatham House, Ramsgate. Mr Neville was also the organist at the parish church. I became fascinated at discovering the intellectual basis on which chords were built up, how a tune could be harmonized in various ways, how the same theme could be introduced at different intervals in contrapuntal music and how the structure of a piece could be traced, just as can the bones of a body without the flesh upon them, or the skeleton of a building without the bricks and mortar over it. I soon realized that if I was to follow this through I needed to know far more about the history of music and the people who wrote and performed it. I had never found it particularly easy to remember dates of wars and battles, but I discovered it was absorbing to trace the history of music, beginning with what is usually thought to be its earliest and simplest form, 'Sumer is icumen in', as a single line or as a canon with four voices following one another at intervals, through to the highly charged and concentrated forms of the twentieth century, particularly Stravinsky. The contrapuntal music of the Elizabethans, the harmonic pieces of the Stuarts, the varied dances, fugal works and choral music of Bach and Handel, the classical sonata form as it was developed from Haydn and Mozart to Beethoven and Schubert, the Romantics of the nineteenth century, including the great symphonists and the programme music of so many of these composers, the operas of Mozart, Rossini and Verdi, and the 'leitmotif', or 'theme' music, of Wagner and Strauss showed me the part musical form can play in the impact a composition makes upon you.

But is it really necessary to know all this in order to enjoy listening to a piece of music? Not at all. No more than it is necessary to know how a building is erected or a picture is painted in order to enjoy looking at them. And if you are just beginning to listen to music, don't bother about trying to understand it. Sit back and let it flow over you. Let it make its own impact on you. If it does have an effect upon you emotionally, or intellectually, you will become interested enough to want to find out more

'Sumer is icumen in', probably the earliest piece of music known in the western world and still the first piece sung by most schoolchildren

about it and in particular, perhaps, more about why and how it
does make its own effect upon you personally. Once you reach
this stage, you will find it easy and natural to understand how a
composer has put the work together, how he has created his
effects and how, in the normal course of events, he has developed
something which has a wholeness about it, a unity, out of the
individual themes from which he started. If you know how a
painter has been able to transfer the impression from his eye to
the canvas, you will find more to enjoy in his painting. If you
appreciate how skilful an architect has been in securing the
balanced proportions his building displays, this will add another
dimension to your appreciation of his work. If you can follow
with the mind, as well as with the ear, the growth of a musical
composition, your appreciation of it will increase with every
performance. It was in just such a way that I was beginning to
listen to orchestral pieces.

I had to do this very largely by means of the 'wireless', as radio
was then called. As a young boy I had listened through earphones
to a crystal set, but by now we possessed a wireless set with a
loudspeaker. At that time the Isle of Thanet was not on the visiting

list of the touring symphony orchestras and I had no opportunity of hearing a live orchestra playing symphonic music near my home. There was, of course, a school orchestra which I often accompanied and sometimes conducted, but this was not as adventurous as the youth orchestras of today and never attempted to play major symphonic works. The BBC was steadily broadcasting its symphony concerts once a week for nine months of the year, and although it sometimes meant using them as background music while preparing for the inevitable school examinations, I was very often able just to sit back and listen. When it came to August and September the radio gave us the Promenade concerts in full measure. Every night, wherever I was, I would try to get within reach of a loudspeaker to listen. But my real objective, of course, was to get to the concerts themselves. I managed to do this for a few nights each season by staying with friends in London who would not mind putting me up and then discovering that I disappeared every evening, very often first to queue and then to stand for a good two hours in the auditorium of the Queen's Hall, feasting on the packed programmes which Sir Henry Wood and his orchestra used to produce.

It was at these Promenade concerts that I first learned most of my orchestral music. The general arrangements then were much simpler than now. One orchestra played throughout the eight weeks. It rehearsed every morning and played every evening. As a result, it was sometimes under-rehearsed, especially with a new work, and by the end of the season was showing signs of exhaustion, though the fervour of the last night always restored the players' adrenalin and made up for some of the more obvious weaknesses which had developed. The main difference, then from now, was that the season was designed to cover all the major works of the great composers from Bach to Elgar and to concentrate many of them in evenings devoted to one composer or, at the most, two at a time. This had the advantage that by listening to a number of works in the same programme we could trace the development of the composer's mind, and, indeed, that by attending on a fixed night each week we could cover most of a composer's orchestral repertoire. For me, Beethoven on Friday was the great night, closely followed by Haydn, Mozart and sometimes Bach, usually on Wednesdays. Tuesdays tended to be a night for new or lesser-known works. Sometimes it was used for English composers alone. Extracts from Wagner operas on Monday nights I found difficult to take. This didn't prevent me from making the attempt but I realize now that I had little or no understanding of either the literary or the musical aspects of Wagner's art. Any impact Monday night at the Proms did make on me came from the swelling mass of sound, rich and luxuriant, sweeping over me, and from the resonant voices of the singers soaring over the tumult. Somehow the stocky figure of Sir Henry Wood, with his characteristic wide-sweeping beat, the surging

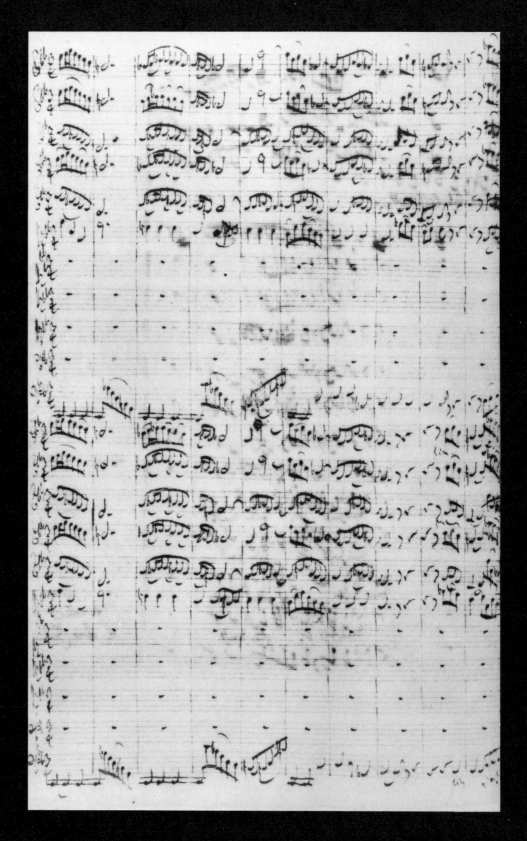

Wagnerian crescendos and the voices battling above them all seemed to be of a piece; but they still did not convert me to Wagner. Indeed, it was another twenty-five years before I began seriously to study him and his work and gradually to find enjoyment in it. Now, where would I be, I wonder, without the splendour of *Die Meistersinger*, the intense joy of *Tristan* and the compulsive music drama of *The Ring*?

I soon discovered a way of persuading the authorities to allow me into the morning rehearsals of the Proms. A letter about my music at school and my intention of becoming a music student initially did the trick and got me a pass. Having once convinced them of this, I was able, by getting round the doorman and then standing at the back and keeping quiet, to slip in on other occasions, a habit which I have continued up to this day. Thus I was able to listen to Sir Henry Wood at work, to watch how he handled the orchestra and soloists and to see how he managed to get through so much in a single rehearsal. It was certainly a businesslike, no-nonsense performance, and from it I learned a great deal, in particular how important it is to know when you go on to the rostrum precisely the time available to each particular item in the programme. It was there, too, that I first realized that it was not enough to know what you wanted; you also had to be able to indicate it clearly to some ninety to a hundred experienced and hardboiled musicians. From then on I never ceased to study the techniques of individual conductors: not content with listening to the finished product, I found it impossible not to watch and analyse at the same time how it was being created.

Sir Henry Wood conducted with a wide, steady beat, feet planted slightly astride and firmly on the rostrum, his body moving with the sound. Compared with some of the gymnastic or ballet-like performances we see today, his would probably be considered dull and rather routine. Yet there was a lesson in it for me. The first requirement of a conductor, especially if he is spending his time with amateur choirs and orchestras, is to be able to give a beat which no one can question. If it can be aesthetic at the same time, so much the better, but what really matters is that the group you are conducting should be held firmly together no matter what happens, given the rhythmic drive essential for the work concerned and led to produce a body of sound which is not only precise but also beautiful.

The Proms today are, of course, in many ways very different from those I have been describing. The BBC performed a great public service when they undertook responsibility for them after Sir Henry Wood's death. It was fortunate that Sir Malcolm Sargent was there, with all his verve and flair, to continue the process of popularizing orchestral music. More recently there has been a wide variety of developments including the presentation of complete operas from Glyndebourne after the season has finished, the inclusion of major choral works such as Bach's

The opening page of the last chorus of Bach's *St Matthew Passion* from a facsimile of the original

St Matthew Passion and Beethoven's Mass in D, and the introduction of a large number of new works, many specially commissioned for the Proms. The burden of the season is now shared among a considerable number of orchestras. This not only lightens the strain and improves the standard of performance, it also gives us the opportunity of hearing the leading provincial orchestras in their own specialities, as well as the other London orchestras besides those of the BBC.

Although the Promenade concerts have been at the Albert Hall since the Queen's Hall was destroyed during the war, today many additional concerts are held in places such as Westminster Cathedral or the Roundhouse, either on Sundays or instead of the normal evening concert. Chamber music and singing by

small choirs are now often included. All this is to the good, but I sometimes wonder whether young people now get from the Proms quite such a solid grounding in the basic works of European music as I and my generation did forty years ago. If not, it is a pity, for there is no better way for the young student to acquire this kind of grounding, and I myself shall always be grateful to the Promenade concerts for playing such a large part in my musical education. I still return when I see an evening or an item which attracts my interest. Now I sit in a box looking at that enthusiastic mass of young people, many of them perhaps hearing these works for the first time. It always brings back many memories of the evenings I have enjoyed down there standing in the prom.

Sir Malcolm Sargent at the last night of the Proms in 1965 with his enthusiastic and devoted Promenaders

One evening, towards the end of my first term at Oxford, I found a note waiting for me on the table in my room. It read quite simply, 'Dear Heath, I am so glad to be able to let you know at once that we elected you tonight to the Organ Scholarship.' It was signed by the Dean, the Rev. M. R. Ridley. I had achieved my objective. From the following autumn I would be organ scholar at Balliol College, responsible for playing Evensong on Sundays and Morning Service at 8 o'clock on weekdays. I would be directly involved in the Balliol concerts held in Hall on each alternate Sunday evening and I could play a more prominent part in the musical life of the university. It meant also that financially life would be somewhat easier. The scholarship – £80 a year – was not one of the most valuable offered by the college, and £80 does not seem a large amount now; but to me in those days it meant a great deal.

I had gone up to Balliol in October 1935 from grammar school as a commoner. For some time I had set my heart on getting to Oxford, and Balliol in particular. As with so many youthful decisions, it is a little difficult at this distance of time to rationalize this one, but having read everything I could get my hands on about Oxford I was attracted by Balliol's intellectual attainments and by the fact that wealth and privilege seemed to carry little weight there. Moreover, Oxford's long connection with those in politics and public life acted as a magnet for me. The fact that I did not succeed in getting an open scholarship in modern subjects meant that I could only take up entrance to the college that had accepted me with the help of a grant from a charitable foundation, a loan from the Kent Education Committee (to be repaid on the completion of my course) and funds from my parents who had to struggle to make the money available. The Balliol organ scholarship enabled me to relieve them of most of the burden they had undertaken and at the same time allowed me to join college and university clubs and take part in their activities. Indeed, I had come up to Balliol knowing that the organ scholarship would become vacant in my first year and determined to do everything possible to keep myself at Oxford by winning it. The previous year I had tried for the organ scholarship at St Catherine's, Cambridge, admittedly rather half-heartedly, and at Keble College, Oxford, without success.

Keble was, in many ways, the Blue Riband of organ scholarships. It was true that Christ Church, New College and Magdalen all had senior organists and choirs of distinction, but Keble had produced many of the leading organists in this country and the Keble scholar was organist of the chapel in his own right. I went to Keble for the examination in some fear and trepidation, for I was young and inexperienced as well as having had insufficient tuition. On such occasions the set pieces are never the main problem, and I did not find the transposition from one key into another – so necessary for lowering the pitch of many of our

'Inside the hall the choir called for peace. In the world outside they were preparing for war'

The Broad Street front of Balliol College, Oxford

hymns and chants so that they can be sung by an undergraduate congregation – too troublesome. I had also had to master the form of accompaniment for plainsong, something I enjoyed immensely, but when it came to improvisation on a theme produced by the examiner, I was at a loss. It was very soon clear to me that I was not going to become organ scholar at Keble. The examiner, kind and considerate, was Dr Thomas Armstrong, himself a former organ scholar of Keble and by then organist at Christ Church and conductor of the Oxford Bach Choir. This was my first meeting with the man who was later to become musical director of the Balliol concerts and whose son, Robert Armstrong, himself no mean musician, was to be my Principal Private Secretary at 10 Downing Street for nearly four years.

After my experience at St Catherine's, Cambridge, and Keble, Oxford, I knew fairly exactly what would be required to get through the examination for an organ scholarship. As soon as I got to Oxford, I concentrated on extra tuition in preparation for the test in December. I took lessons twice a week from the organist at St Aldate's, and I was able to practise on the splendid three-manual modern instrument there. I also practised on the organ in Balliol because I knew all the competitors would be asked to play on it, and there was therefore some advantage in getting used to it, particularly as it was an old two-manual instrument with tracker action, stops which were heavy to pull out, and a straight pedal board, rather than the modern fan-shaped pedal board, all of which were hazards for the unsuspecting. When the day for the examination came, I concentrated on four pieces. The

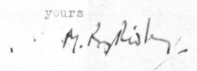

BALLIOL COLLEGE,
OXFORD.

Dear Heath

I am so glad to be able to let you know at once t
we elected you to night to the Organ Scholarship.

yours

first was Bach's Prelude in E Flat, commonly called 'St Anne', based on the tune which is well known as that for the first line of the hymn 'O God our help in ages past'. The second was one of the trio sonatas of Bach. Simple as those may seem, with a single line of notes from each hand on a different manual and the feet on the pedal board, they are, as every organist knows, amongst the most difficult of works to play effectively. Thirdly I chose Mendelssohn's Sonata No. 2 in C Minor, a splendid work which had always been a favourite of mine, as well as of the organist of St Peter's-in-Thanet, and, finally, a quiet piece by Vaughan Williams, based on the Welsh tune 'Rhosymedre'. In addition, I was well prepared to carry out the transposition of hymn tunes and chants and, if necessary, some improvisation.

The examiner was Dr Ernest Walker, one of Oxford's most interesting musical characters. Slightly stooping, well bearded, with a high voice and piercing laugh, I had seen him at the Balliol concerts with his friends the two Deneke sisters. For many years he had been director of the concerts and never failed to appear at them. In chapel, he asked me to play the Mendelssohn Sonata, but stopped me before I could embark on the build-up of the fugue in the last movement, saying he wanted to hear the Vaughan Williams. After that he listened to the whole of the Bach St Anne fugue. I did some transposition and that was that. He seemed pleased. I kept clear of everyone while the other competitors were playing. It was only when I got the note on my table the same evening that I knew of my success. I was glad they had decided so quickly.

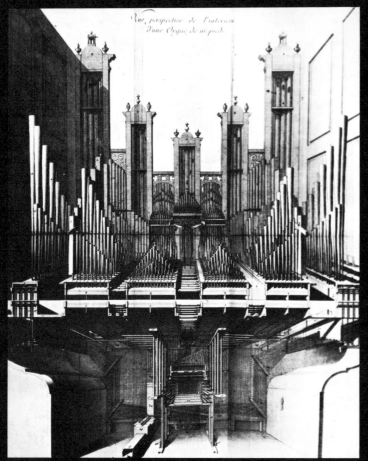

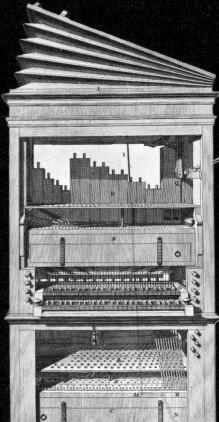

The Splendour of Organs

Above: Contemporary engravings of the inside workings of organs of the eighteenth century (left) and seventeenth century (right).

Left: The organ in the Holywell Music Room Oxford

Opposite: Exterior of the organ (completed in 1750) in the abbey at Weingarthen en Souabe

Décoration extérieure en perspective de l'Orgue de l'Abbaye de Weingarthen, dans la Souabe en Allemagne.

Fait et fini le 24 Juin 1750, par M.ᵉ Gabler M.ᵗʳᵉ Facteur d'Orgues de la Ville de Ravensbourg dans le même Pays.

Echelle de 5 Toises.

After I had been elected organ scholar of Balliol I got to know Ernest Walker well. From time to time he would invite me to tea at his home in north Oxford, a typical Victorian house with heavy furniture and a rather gloomy interior. There he would discuss the college concerts and what was being performed at the Holywell Music Room, in which I was now taking a considerable interest. What I enjoyed most, however, was listening to his recollections of musicians and performances. He had known Brahms, and even possessed some of Brahms's original manuscripts, which he allowed me to see. He was, to me, a link between contemporary music and one of the great symphonists of all time.

It was through Ernest Walker that my interest in Brahms was first seriously aroused, and I soon began to concentrate my attention on his symphonies, beginning with the Fourth, his last. For most people this is less formidable than the First Symphony. Its romantic opening, with drooping strings, followed by an upward answer, the simple horn tune of the second movement, and the vibrant Scherzo leading into the splendour of the last movement based on an oft-repeated theme, all gave me intense enjoyment. I listened to it innumerable times on records. For the newcomer it is the last movement which is difficult to understand, but even without detailed knowledge of the structure one cannot help but be carried away as the mass of sound builds up to its climax. By its nature, it can never be an anti-climax; it is the crowning achievement of the work.

Brahms's First Symphony I got to know when Toscanini brought the BBC Symphony Orchestra to play in the New Theatre at Oxford. Toscanini had just begun to conduct again in England. It was always said that he would only conduct the BBC Symphony Orchestra, and then seldom outside London. For us in Oxford it was a remarkable event. The intensity of his performance and his long, wide beat remain vividly in my memory, together with the spaciousness of his treatment of this work. As Toscanini launched into the major theme of the last movement, warm and vigorous, I felt a deep emotion welling within me. He made me feel that everything that had come before had been a preparation for this – the mark of a totally satisfying performance.

Since then, I have come to love the freshness and spontaneity of the Third Symphony; the glorious exuberance of its opening, the simplicity of the slow movement, the sad lilt of the third movement, and the forceful jollity of the leaping tune of the last. I wish it were played more often. The Second Symphony I have heard on innumerable occasions; it is the one which now makes the least impact on me. Perhaps Brahms was drained after the immense effort involved in creating the First. It seems to me to be lacking in depth.

It used to be fashionable to criticize Brahms because of his lack of orchestral colour. It is certainly true that he did not use his

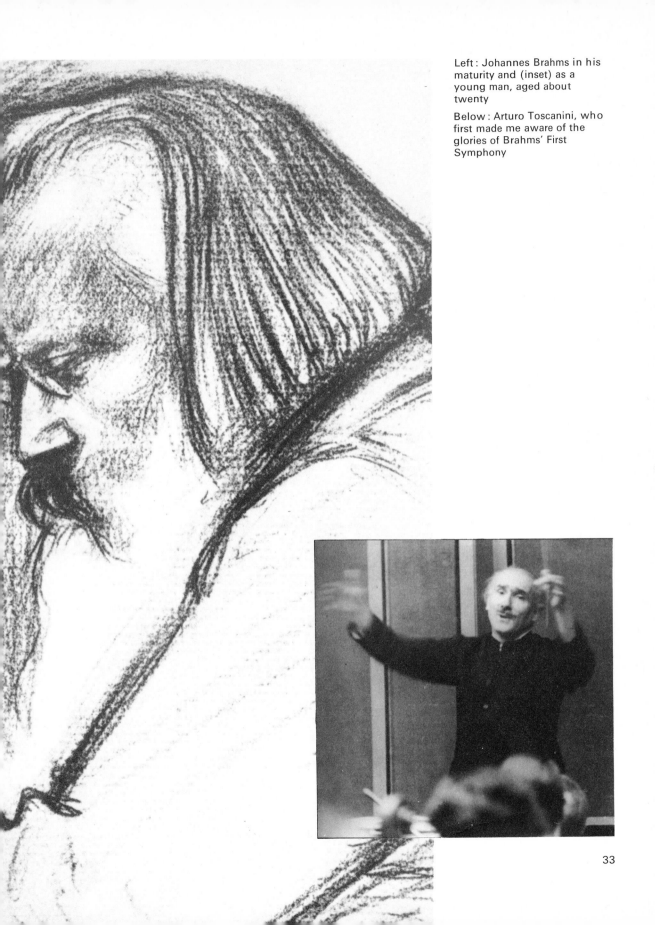

Left : Johannes Brahms in his maturity and (inset) as a young man, aged about twenty

Below : Arturo Toscanini, who first made me aware of the glories of Brahms' First Symphony

palette for the purpose of showing off orchestral technique, but there are few glories like the glory of a full orchestra playing the last movement of Brahms's First Symphony. As with all great composers, he was able to express the whole gamut of human emotion, but, above all, I found that he was able to write music which expressed the sheer joy of being alive. Nothing does this better than one of his early works, the Serenade in A. How often have I played the recording of that delightful piece made under Pablo Casals at the Marlboro Festival, set in the heart of the wooded hills of Vermont, while sitting at Chequers on a summer evening looking out on the peaceful English countryside.

Brahms, too, is a marvellous composer for group music-making. Take for example the first set of waltzes, which were written to be played with four hands on one piano. The second and third sets of waltzes, the *Liebeslieder*, were similarly written with a vocal quartet added to sing the setting of these love songs. They were meant to be played and sung in the home, but how seldom that happens today. It is not the same when it becomes a public performance.

I was once taken by surprise by the intimacy of music-making in public when I heard Myra Hess play Brahms's First Piano Concerto in D Minor with Dimitri Mitropoulos conducting the New York Philharmonic Orchestra in 1955 on one of its visits to the Festival Hall in London. The piano part of Brahms's First Concerto is fiendish, but it is not intended as a showpiece for the soloist's technique. It is only when the technical difficulties can be overcome and taken in their stride that pianists can begin to convey the depths of Brahms's music in the Concerto. It then appears extraordinarily simple. That night, in the Festival Hall, I suddenly realized that Myra Hess, Mitropoulos and the New York Philharmonic were just making music together; as an audience we might just as well not have been there. She was totally involved in the beauty of Brahms; he stood beside her in an ill-fitting tail coat and baggy trousers, his long arms by his side, hardly moving; the orchestra at one with both of them. There was no attempt to show off; Brahms was simply allowed to speak for himself through the piano and the orchestra. That was a night to remember.

The Deneke sisters, Margaret and Helena, close friends of Ernest Walker, were among those most active in Oxford musical life. Whenever I went to their house in Norham Gardens, in north Oxford, I knew that there would be musicians of interest to meet: either the great going to play in Lady Margaret Hall, where Helena was a Fellow, or yet another young prodigy – pianist, violinist or cellist – whom Margaret was helping to get established. Of the great, the one I wanted to meet was Sir Donald Tovey. He had been the first composition scholar at Balliol and had become for us a legend in his own lifetime. His work as conductor of the Reid Orchestra in Edinburgh was widely admired. His compositions, some of which the critics found 'too eclectic', with their obvious debt to the Romantics, were less appreciated, but it was believed that if he had chosen he could have been the greatest pianist of his time. One Sunday afternoon, when I went up to the Denekes for tea, I found Tovey there; alas, his hands were badly crippled from arthritis. Nevertheless, he sat and played for us. Despite his infirmity, his deep understanding of the music came through to us in that small group sitting around the drawing room. He produced a beautiful tone; he made the piano sing in a way which was remarkable. He refused to play on anything except a Bösendorfer, a piano noted for its soft tonal quality. I can still picture him sitting quietly on that piano stool, a large, burly figure with a craggy head, producing that lovely tone. How I wish I had heard him in his prime.

Donald Tovey made his most enduring contribution to music with his *Essays in Musical Analysis*, largely based on programme notes he wrote for his own orchestral concerts in Edinburgh. As the years pass Tovey's writings will have less and less strictly contemporary relevance, but his analyses of the works of his own generation as well as of the past are invaluable for those who want to have a deeper appreciation of all aspects of music. Indeed I would go so far as to say that no other written work of this kind can give one a greater understanding of music, written as they are in elegant style, full of witticisms and dotted with stimulating verbal illustrations.

Tovey died twenty years before Bruckner's and Mahler's great rise to popularity in Europe and America during the fifties and sixties, although, as we shall see, he partly foresaw it. At Oxford, we had just begun to discover the delights of Bruckner and the excitement of Mahler. It was Bruckner's Fourth Symphony that I stumbled upon first, on a recording which I constantly played. It had a freshness and spontaneity about it – perhaps now I would say a little naivety – which conveyed to me the real joy of music-making. Of course it is a long work but I have never quibbled at that in music. For us in the thirties, threatened as we were by dictatorship and war, Bruckner seemed to bring something reassuring from the world of nature into our lives. In many ways Bruckner's Fourth appeared to be a continuation of Schubert's Great C Major Symphony. Later, after the war, I pursued the rest of Bruckner's works, until I experienced the strength and splendour of the Seventh and Eighth Symphonies. If Bruckner's Fourth is still the most popular of his symphonies, without doubt the Seventh and Eighth are the greatest. The Adagio in the Seventh builds up into the most powerful and emotional movements in his music. Bruckner considered his finest work to be the *Te Deum*, and it is significant that at the culmination of this personal expression of faith, to the words, '*Non confundar in aeternum*', he reintroduces the theme of the Adagio of the Seventh Symphony.

I got to know Mahler through *Das Lied von der Erde*, never more beautifully sung than by Kathleen Ferrier. Compared with Bruckner this was strange music indeed, but it had its own fascination. Nature is strongly present in Mahler, too, but here it is felt as a hideous torment contrasting with spiky cheerfulness. In the sixties I became preoccupied with Mahler's symphonies; each is part of the development of a sustained philosophy yet each varies greatly in its structure, material and final impact. The best advice I can give to the listener unfamiliar with Mahler is to follow the composer's own progression from the First Symphony onwards. Every conductor today seems to have a different idea of what Mahler wanted, but I know of nothing better than the few existing recordings by Bruno Walter, who himself worked with Mahler and knew his mind.

But to return to Donald Tovey. In his essay on Mahler's Fourth Symphony, written in the thirties, he showed a perception of both Bruckner and Mahler, combined with an acute understanding of our own musical approach and taste, which I find quite astonishing for the time at which it was written. In the midst of a brilliant piece Donald Tovey says: 'We do not wish it generally known, but we would all like to write like Mahler if we dared; and we all think that we could. The martyr whom he most nearly resembles is Bruckner but Mahler is anything but helpless and raises none of the sympathy of a naive artist struggling for self expression. Far from it. We find his facility deadly.' Later

Anton Bruckner (below) and Gustav Mahler: a contrast in men and conducting styles. Contemporary silhouettes by Dr O. Boehler

he sums up his views by writing: 'The musical culture of Great Britain will probably be the better for the rise of a vogue for Bruckner and Mahler; and perhaps Mahler will do so more than Bruckner, because his mastery will discourage the cult of amateurish things which keeps us contented with ignorance and ready to believe that ineptitude is noble in itself; and the good taste which is ready to take offence at Mahler's sentimentality will be all the better for being shocked.' What foresight, what an understanding of the British musical sensibility at that time, what wise advice. What Tovey foresaw has come to pass, and I have no doubt that our musical culture is all the better for it.

There was little chance of hearing performances of either Bruckner or Mahler during my time at Oxford. Their works appeared seldom at the Proms. No doubt the scale of the forces required for Mahler in particular, especially for his Eighth Symphony, the 'Symphony of a Thousand', accounted in some measure for this, and the inadequacy of rehearsal time compounded the difficulties; but I doubt whether either composer was much in keeping with Henry Wood's musical outlook. What a contrast with the Prom in 1963, when I heard Stokowski – he was already over eighty – conducting the London Symphony Orchestra in Mahler's Second Symphony, the 'Resurrection'. It was a superb performance in the Stokowski manner, rich, warm and vibrant. At the end the crowded promenade went wild with excitement. To their delight, Stokowski returned and, after a performance which would have exhausted almost any other conductor, picked up his baton and played the second half of the last movement again. On only one other occasion have I ever heard part of a work played again as an encore. That was when Giulini conducted the New Philharmonia Choir and Orchestra in the Verdi Requiem at Parma in 1963 for the celebration of the 150th anniversary of Verdi's birth. After a scintillating performance of the Sanctus, the excited audience refused to allow the work to proceed. Giulini had no alternative but to repeat the Sanctus. To the British, such an explosion of spontaneous feeling in the middle of a Requiem Mass, and followed at that by a repetition of the Sanctus, would have been completely incomprehensible; but to the Italians it was a perfectly natural outpouring of their joy and delight not only in a magical piece of musical writing but also in a meticulous yet inspiring performance of it.

Nor did the orchestras coming to Oxford bring Bruckner and Mahler with them. If anything it was Sibelius whose virtues were proclaimed, whose works were more and more widely performed. His Second Symphony, much akin to its Romantic predecessors, with its wide, sweeping tunes and orthodox orchestration, was already popular. In the Town Hall at Oxford I heard his Fifth Symphony, whose electrifying climax had everyone on their feet at the end cheering. Sir Thomas Beecham brought the Royal Philharmonic Orchestra to play Sibelius's Seventh Symphony, all

English-born Leopold Stokowski, aged eighty-five; he had wonderfully expressive hands

in one movement, a great favourite of his, at the Sheldonian Theatre. That was more difficult to understand at first hearing but with repetition it became clear how Sibelius's mind was moving. Now Sibelius is unfashionable but no doubt in time that will change too.

It was not until I got to Boston on a debating tour of the United States in December 1939 that I heard Mahler in the flesh, so to speak. There, in that resonant Symphony Hall, the home of the Boston Symphony Orchestra, I heard Koussevitzky conduct the Adagio from Mahler's Ninth Symphony. It was an intensely moving experience to hear Koussevitzky draw such a depth of tone from the strings and to listen to the mild-toned brass blending in so warmly. Yet, looking back, I find myself asking how one of the world's greatest conductors, with a superb orchestral instrument at his command, could have extracted just one movement from a Mahler symphony for performance in a concert programme. Would he have done it with the Adagio of Beethoven's Ninth? Or of Brahms's Second? Or of Elgar's First? I do not think so. Even in 1939, there was still something strange about the way Mahler was treated.

As soon as I had settled in at Balliol, I applied to join the Oxford Bach Choir. After an audition, which was very largely a question of sight-reading and deciding which sort of voice I had got, I was accepted as a first bass. The choir met for rehearsal every Monday in the lecture theatre at the University Museum, a big room with seats steeply raked to the back. The conductor stood where the lecturer would normally have been and just in front of him was a piano with the accompanist. I soon found that it was not just a case of being a member of the choir; there was a marked tendency to form smaller groups within the choir as a whole. Perhaps the Balliol group was particularly clannish in this; at any rate we always made a point of sitting together on the topmost bench, the basses on the right facing the conductor and the tenors on the left. The sopranos and altos, from the women's colleges and from the city and its surrounding villages, were on either side of us. One thing which contributed to the Balliol men remaining together as a group was that we were invited each Sunday morning to the house of one of our Senior Fellows, Cyril Bailey, a most distinguished Latin scholar and writer, to practise the bass and tenor parts on our own. At these private mini-rehearsals I was expected both to sing and to accompany at the same time.

The Finnish composer Jan Sibelius. He will become increasingly recognized as one of the great symphonists of the twentieth century

In my first term we were rehearsing Vaughan Williams's 'Sea' Symphony, a work with which the Oxford Bach Choir felt it had a particular connection. Although the first performance at Leeds had not been a conspicuous success, the second, at Oxford, was a triumph. Vaughan Williams is said to have written in Sir Hugh Allen's score: 'I thought I had written an unsingable work but tonight you have sung it magnificently.' For me it is one of Vaughan Williams's most effective compositions. It thrilled me from the beginning. Its exciting opening, a short vigorous trumpet declaration, followed by the sudden, dramatic entry of the choir, 'Behold the sea itself . . .', sounds as the choir resolves the opening chords like a great wave just on the point of breaking. It rolls over and then comes the swell of the rollers 'and on its limitless, heaving breast, the ships'. The slow movement conveys that feeling of limitless space and time one knows so well at sea, that feeling of unity in the world. The Scherzo, the dancing waves shimmering and twinkling in the sun, is a far from easy movement for a big choir to carry out with precision and the necessary lightness of tone. Diction, too, is a problem, at the speed required here. In contrast, the last movement brings peace: there are some who feel that Vaughan Williams develops it at too great a length but so heavenly is its last theme, particularly when sung by the soprano and baritone soloists, 'O! We can wait no longer, we too take ship, O soul', that I find it entirely acceptable. Walt Whitman's words, used by Vaughan Williams, are amongst the most moving he ever wrote. For me, the 'Sea' Symphony was not some passing phenomenon: I have come to love it more and more as the years

Sir Hugh Allen, deemed for thirty years the most influential man in British music

have gone by. It comes constantly into my mind when sailing and I realize how well Vaughan Williams was able to express the feel of the sea. When, after a day's racing on the Solent, *Morning Cloud* is one of an apparently endless series of boats of every size, shape and kind, all returning from their pleasure to their moorings, Whitman's words 'a motley procession with many a fleck of foam' seems particularly appropriate to us all.

The Bach Choir's plans to sing the 'Sea' Symphony early in 1936 were interrupted by the sudden death of King George V in January that year. When we got back for the beginning of term we found that it had been decided that the choir should sing the *German Requiem* by Brahms in the Sheldonian Theatre as a memorial to the late King. We had just ten days in which to rehearse this work. The older members of the choir of course already knew it well, but for the great majority of us it was the first time we had ever sung it. Sir Hugh Allen, the Heather Professor of Music at Oxford at that time, was returning to conduct us. He was the doyen of Oxford musicians and had established a national reputation for his performance of this work.

Sir Hugh was well known to my generation of students by repute as a remarkable though somewhat fearsome man. After becoming a church organist at the age of eleven in his home town of Reading, he was appointed assistant organist at Chichester Cathedral. There he indulged his love of the sea, which remained with him all his life, and bought his first boat. He went on to be organ scholar at Christ's College, Cambridge. It is said that when he first arrived at the college he told the cab to wait, saying to the porter at the lodge, 'Don't move my bags. I want to look round to see if I like this place first.' He then went straight on to be organist at St Asaph Cathedral in Wales, then at Ely Cathedral, and later became organist at New College, Oxford. For many years he was both Director of the Royal College of Music in London and Professor of Music in Oxford. For more than a quarter of a century he was conductor of the Oxford Bach Choir. During this time he not only built up the choir into a sound musical instrument, he also established a reputation for wit, although with a somewhat caustic tongue. We looked forward eagerly to his appearance at the first rehearsal. He immediately took a grip on the situation and drove us relentlessly. As we had so few rehearsals he kept us much later than usual at night, so much so that on one occasion some of the ladies tried to slip out quietly and unobtrusively down the side of the lecture hall to catch their last bus home. Suddenly spotting this, Sir Hugh stopped everything, threw his baton to the floor, put his hands on his hips and glared at the unfortunate women as now, with all eyes upon them, they stumbled far from silently down the steps. Then, looking up at Cyril Bailey, probably the senior member of the choir and sitting among the basses, he exploded: 'Good God, Cyril, they are the same women creeping out now who crept out

Vaughan Williams at the time
of the first performance of his
Fifth Symphony

fifty years ago!' It was after some such similar occasion that Sir
Hugh, walking to the Music School in the Clarendon Building,
found himself confronted by an irate lady who stopped him in his
tracks and said, very forcefully, 'Sir Hugh, you must not go on
being so rude to the altos', to which Sir Hugh replied without
pausing: 'Madam, those whom the Lord loveth, them also he
chasteneth', and passed on.

The final rehearsal for the *Requiem* was held on the Sunday
morning of the performance. The Balliol contingent, with its
usual farsightedness, had decided to occupy the front row in the
Sheldonian because it appeared to be the only place where the
wooden benches were covered with cushions. We soon learned
our mistake; Sir Hugh tapped his baton and said: 'You can put
away all those copies, you must know it by heart now.' The rest
of the choir discreetly lowered their copies behind other people's
backs. We had to put ours down in front of us and manage with
surreptitious glances from time to time.

It was the second movement which gave him the greatest
difficulty. The timpanist could not meet Sir Hugh's exacting
demands for a relentless dotted rhythm in 'All flesh doth perish
as the grass'. 'One last go,' said Sir Hugh ominously, 'and just
watch me.' He started again and then, with eyes fixed purpose-
fully on the face of the timpanist, he marched menacingly through
the orchestra, step by step, beat by beat, towards this wretched
creature now cowering lower and lower over his kettledrums. We,
too, watched petrified as Sir Hugh, now hammering the dotted
beat with his fist into the hollow of his hand, finally achieved the
result he wanted. Never, before or since, have I seen intimidation
used to such good effect.

Franz Joseph Haydn, whose vast output of chamber music, choral works and symphonies provides so much enjoyment to all who love music

Sir Hugh's conception of the Brahms Requiem had spaciousness and dignity, delicacy and at the same time intensity; it was never rushed or forced, but had all the assurance and balance which stems from a deep understanding of the work. From the quiet, perfectly sustained chords of the opening, 'Blest are they that mourn', the rhythmic intensity of 'All flesh doth perish as the grass', the fervent build-up to 'Death where is thy sting?' – surely one of the most splendid harmonic progressions in choral music – and the two great fugues, interspersed with the soaring soprano solo, 'Ye who now sorrow', through to the final chords of the Requiem as they die away, all this he knit into one imposing structure. The impact on me that Sunday afternoon was lasting. From the many performances I have heard since I have learned, rather sadly, one thing. I have never gained as much satisfaction from hearing the Brahms Requiem or playing recordings of it as I did from that one occasion on which I rehearsed and sang it. In fact this feeling of mine applies not only to the Brahms; but to almost every work in which I have sung. It may be that the mere physical act of singing provides an outlet for the emotional content of the work which cannot be obtained by sitting in a concert hall or room and listening to it. It may also be that, having identified oneself closely with a work as a result of singing it, the difficulty of appreciating other performances becomes that much greater.

I sang two other major works with the Bach Choir whilst I was at Oxford, Haydn's *The Seasons* and Beethoven's *Missa Solemnis*. *The Seasons* is an enchanting work, too little performed in this country. Haydn maintains the classical form both in the solo arias and in the choruses, which have a strength and beauty of their own; but what makes the work so delightful, both to listen to and to sing, is the way the orchestral accompaniment illustrates and illuminates the text in musical terms. One of the best examples of this is in the bass aria 'Behold along the dewy grass, in search of scent the spaniel roves'. As he does so you visualize his nose moving from side to side; and when 'The startled fowl flies instant up', we hear him go winging skyward. Of course, no orchestral instrument can give a perfect imitation of a bird flying or a dog sniffing around, though some electronic instruments and in the old days the Wurlitzer cinema organs have attempted to do so. What instruments can do is to give an indication in recognizable musical language of what is going on. Haydn's language in this respect is very simple, as is Beethoven's in the 'Pastoral' Symphony.

When we come to Beethoven's Mass in D we are dealing with a very different sort of work. Here Beethoven was struggling to express the depths of emotion which lay within him. The struggle is all too obvious in large stretches of the work, a struggle which reflects itself in the difficulties which face any choir singing it. It requires, I believe, a relentless drive to stand any chance of recreating Beethoven's efforts to reach the sublime. The effect cannot ever be achieved by a choir which is itself struggling. Paradoxically, the choir needs to be able to produce even more than Beethoven demanded; it is only then, with an intense impetus from the conductor, that the work can make its impact. Even when Beethoven grants us a brief respite, such as in the lovely Benedictus with the solo violin obbligato, the work must always be moving forward right up to its last passionate demand for peace, '*Dona nobis pacem*'. Some think that the work has a good many rough edges; in my view it is quite wrong to smooth them out. This was at the heart of a discussion I had with Giulini one day at the Edinburgh Festival and again later when he came to 10 Downing Street, while he was preparing for a performance of the Mass in St Paul's Cathedral. His is a beautifully controlled performance in which the quality of the soloists, choir and orchestra is always happily balanced, but for me it is not Beethoven. In the process, the rough edges have been smoothed out. For me the Mass epitomizes man's struggle through life and at the end it is a *demand* for peace, not peace itself, which remains.

In addition to the Haydn and Beethoven we also learned two smaller Bach works, 'Sing to the Lord a new song' and 'Jesu, priceless treasure', which we sang in the chapel of St George's, Windsor, a new experience from the point of view of acoustics. As an organ scholar, I was taken up into the organ loft by the chapel organist, W. H. – later Sir William – Harris, so that I could see the double console there. The two consoles were identical and placed at right angles to each other to form an 'L'. This enabled duets to be played on the organ, though there are remarkably few works, to my knowledge, written in this form. One console could, of course, have been used to provide the orchestral accompaniment for the other when works such as Handel's organ concertos, for example, were being played. Although obviously great fun for organists who might want to do this or to improvise an echo piece in which each answered the other, it was a somewhat extravagant arrangement. When the organ at St George's was rebuilt recently, one console was removed and the organ assumed the normal form. I have not seen any other organ in the world which had two consoles arranged in this way. There are, of course, many instances in churches and cathedrals where the main console is near the organ and where there is a replica of it in the nave, so that the organist can be close to the choir and congregation on some festive occasion. There are a number of cathedrals where, in addition to the main organ, there is a small chamber or pipe organ available in another part of the cathedral to accompany the choir. In the chapel of the Escorial, the former palace of the kings of Spain, outside Madrid, I found three organs, each of equal importance, one at the west end, one at the north and one at the south. I played the one at the south side, a magnificent baroque instrument, but I must confess I found it difficult to see how the three could be used together.

Until I went up to Oxford I had had little opportunity of hearing any chamber music. What a horrible phrase that is. Mention it on radio or television and the switch will immediately be turned to another channel. The mere sight of the words on a programme is enough to make anyone run a mile, resolving to have nothing whatever to do with this strange art, which conjures up in the mind pictures of scraping fiddles and cellos in quartets, or of sopranos warbling at interminable length without an apparent tune – and what is more, in other people's languages – or, perhaps worst of all, of over-stretched tenors failing to cope adequately with the thrashing chords of an overweening accompanist. Yet all 'chamber music' means is music to be played in the home or in the music room of a large house. Some of the most personal music ever written was composed for a trio, often a violin, a cello and a piano, or a string trio of violin, cello and viola, occasionally for three wind instruments or for individual combinations of instruments which composers fancied. Very often the pieces were written for particular artists, or groups of friends, and usually the composer played one of the instruments himself. The songs of Schubert, Schumann and Brahms, and in our own day Benjamin Britten, are among the most effective expressions of musical ideas, and as such they frequently depict the most intimate of human emotions – joy and sorrow, love, despair and death. Some contemporary music in this field may be difficult to comprehend, though not necessarily any more so than other music of our time, but the chamber works of Haydn and Mozart, Beethoven and Schubert, Schumann and Brahms for the most part make an immediate appeal. This is particularly true of the string quartets of Haydn and Mozart. For those who are thinking of exploring this kind of music, Beethoven's early quartets are attractive but they develop structurally and harmonically until his last quartets, amongst the finest ever written, become difficult to appreciate fully without sustained thought and repeated listening. At the end of his novel *Point Counter Point* Aldous Huxley leaves his principal character to die after putting on a record of the slow movement of Beethoven's next but last quartet. It is true that this work has a quality of finality which only Beethoven achieved. I often wonder, however, whether Huxley's man would not have more peacefully left this earth if the record had been playing the final pages of Beethoven's last piano sonata in C minor.

It was at the Balliol Sunday evening concerts that I learned most of my chamber music. These concerts, held on every alternate Sunday evening during term in the college hall, had been started in 1885. Benjamin Jowett was the first Master of Balliol to encourage an interest in music in the college. He brought John Farmer from Harrow to Balliol to be Director of Music. John Farmer was very largely responsible for the compilation of the book of Harrow Songs, many of which he composed himself. Later, he put together a similar book of Balliol Songs.

Jelly d'Aranyi at the time she was playing at the Balliol concerts for my generation

John Farmer started the Musical Society at Balliol. The first programmes, rather like the first Promenade concerts, contained a considerable number of small individual items of a mixed variety. Gradually they moved towards their present format of a trio or quartet, normally playing two or three pieces, or a singer with piano accompanist in three or four groups of songs. One concert a term was set aside for a performance by members of the university. Most of the concerts were packed. The atmosphere was informal, with only the first third of the hall occupied by rows of chairs; in the remaining space people sat on tables and benches or anything else which was available, sometimes having to make do with the floor. These concerts had one tradition which no other college maintained. At the end of the concert, when the applause to the final item was dying, the Master, sitting in his corner chair in the front row, waved his programme aloft. The whole audience rose, faced the organ at the back of the hall and sang the chorale printed on the programme sheet. It gave the

concert a tremendous finale. The organ at that time was hand-pumped and when the hall was full, the chorale long and splendid, it was a very exhausted and sweat-bedevilled 'scout', or college servant, who emerged from the side of the organ as we all disappeared into the night. When I go to a Balliol concert now, I automatically turn round at the end, expecting to hear the chorale tune blazing forth; but the tradition has lapsed, and we just shuffle out like any other audience anywhere else.

At the Balliol concerts I heard for the first time many of the major works for trios, quartets and quintets, as well as song cycles for the voice. Many performances return to delight my memory, such as Beethoven's 'Archduke' Trio, surely one of the loveliest ever written. How many times since have I returned home late at night exhausted after a tiring day at the House of Commons; how many times have I gone up to my flat at 10 Downing Street, after a tempestuous day of meetings of every kind, and put on the recording of the 'Archduke'. Its very first bars bring a calmness and repose which restore tranquillity to the troubled mind. Beethoven's first 'Razumovsky' Quartet, which I also first heard at Balliol, I find robust and intellectually stimulating, with its glorious melody in the first movement bracing one for sterner things to come, while Schubert's B Flat Trio is still sheer joy, bubbling champagne, flowing along and carrying one with it whatever the difficulties of the day may be. Twice in Hall I heard the complete song cycle *Dichterliebe* by Schumann – both unforgettable occasions. There were frequently individual songs by the Lieder composers but the *Dichterliebe* has always had a special place in my heart.

The concert performance at Balliol I shall remember above all was given by Jelly d'Aranyi and Adila Fachiri, accompanied on the piano by Sydney Watson in a superb rendering of Bach's Concerto for Two Violins in D Minor. The two sisters were already renowned for their performance of this piece, and never before or since, not even with the Oistrakhs, father and son, have I heard the slow movement, one violin answering another, so beautifully phrased and sustained. One did not miss the orchestral accompaniment. At the end there was a happy scene as, with all tension released, both sisters simultaneously threw their arms round Sydney Watson's neck and uninhibitedly kissed him.

This was an occasion with a special meaning for Balliol, for Ernest Walker had once brought Joachim, the greatest violinist of his day and a friend of Brahms, to Balliol to play at the concerts in Hall, and Joachim in his turn had brought the sisters, actually his great-nieces, to Balliol to give their first performances in England as girl prodigies. It was at the college concerts that they had made their reputation nearly thirty years before, and now they had returned to play for the next generation. It was a wonderfully moving experience of continuity in our music-making.

Balliol College Musical Society

1000th Concert

Sunday, November 28th, 1937

at 9.30 p.m.

———

ERNEST WALKER   WILLIAM H. HARRIS

VICTOR HELY-HUTCHINSON   SYDNEY WATSON

THE OXFORD CHAMBER ORCHESTRA

THE BALLIOL CHORAL SOCIETY
Conductor: E. R. G. HEATH.

My main contribution to the concerts was to create the Balliol Choir to which tenors and basses came from the college with a handful from Trinity, next door, and the sopranos and altos came from Somerville and Lady Margaret Hall with reinforcements from the other women's colleges. Our big opportunity came when we had the Thousandth Concert in 1937. Everyone taking part had to have some connection with Balliol. We sang Handel's coronation anthem, 'Zadok the Priest' and then the 'Songs from England's Helicon' by Ernest Walker, who paced up and down the back of the hall during rehearsals. These little-known pieces can be sung either by a quartet or octet or a full choir. They combine a sensibility and vigour, harmonic elegance and balanced structure which make them perfect examples of this miniature art form. The harmonic progressions are tricky and they are not easy to sing well. The accompaniment requires a good pianist; maybe it is even better played on two pianos. We were fortunate in having George Malcolm at the piano, the composition scholar at Balliol at the same time as I was organ scholar. He had a brilliant technique and a fabulous memory for music. To him everything seemed to come easily and I envied him his facility.

Ernest Walker and Victor Hely-Hutchinson, a former composition scholar at the college and Professor of Music at Birmingham, now remembered for his pastiche of Handel in his setting of 'Old Mother Hubbard', played Bach's C Major Concerto for Two Pianos. Ernest Walker had the strange characteristic of always playing his left hand slightly before the right – so unusual was this, that, it was said irreverently and probably apocryphally, it was recorded in the medical text books – the result being that the concerto became something of a scramble as his right hand tried to keep up with his left and Victor Hely-Hutchinson tried to keep up with both; it was certainly an exciting performance. William Harris and Sydney Watson played Donald Tovey's 'Balliol Dances' for four hands on one piano, reminiscent of the well-known waltzes by Brahms. In order to carry out the undertaking about college connections, Cyril Bailey announced in a charming speech at the end of the concert that 'both Bach and Handel had been made Honorary Fellows for the evening'.

Later, in the fifties and sixties, I was able to repay some of the debt I owed to the Balliol concerts by persuading others to play there. Yehudi and Hephzibah Menuhin played together three Beethoven sonatas, concluding with the 'Kreutzer'. They had a rapturous reception which seemed to stun even them. Claudio Arrau played a monumental programme of Liszt. This time it was the audience who seemed to be taken aback. Only then did I realize that fresh generations of Oxford men had become accustomed to a delicate and – as I would describe – anaemic kind of performance, the sort of playing which Smeterlin produced for my generation in the Mozart G Major Sonata. To hear Liszt played in a massive, scintillating way, was to those students a revelation of how a great pianist can make the piano sound. It took me back to the concert which Rachmaninov had played at the New Theatre at Oxford in 1938. He, too, was one of the great masters of the piano. He included in his programme four of Chopin's Studies; the last, in which he swept up and down the keyboard with fingers apparently of steel, absolutely accurate and brilliantly under control, remains my most vivid memory of that concert. Of course the famous Rachmaninov Prelude in C Sharp Major was produced as an encore and played without sentimentality. Not for him, the composer, the folklore about the piece depicting the Kremlin bells sounding. For him it was one of his preludes, perfectly shaped, properly balanced, never to be played perfunctorily or romantically, but another miniature to be meticulously executed.

Sergei Rachmaninov, one of the greatest pianists of his time, whose orchestral works are becoming more and more popular

Another aspect of music with which I became involved was providing music for plays, in particular the Balliol Players and the Oxford University Dramatic Society, OUDS. The Balliol Players were a group who went on tour with a Greek play at the end of the summer term. It was very pleasant, after a strenuous academic year, to spend ten days moving through Oxfordshire, Berkshire, down to the west country and then back to London, putting on the play once or twice a day. It was almost always performed in the open air, so to a certain extent we were at the mercy of the weather. I was asked to write the music for *The Acharnians* by Aristophanes. I was helped by Walt Rostow, later to become Foreign Affairs Adviser at the White House to President Johnson. At the end of the spring term of 1939, I also did some arrangements for the OUDS production of *The Taming of the Shrew*.

By this time I was president of the Oxford Union Debating Society, for politics was my other love at the university, together with music. In arranging a programme of debates at the Union, I sought Sir Hugh Allen's help to persuade Sir Thomas Beecham to come down for the main debate of the term, the Presidential Debate. With his help everything was arranged. Sir Thomas, who was already well known, if not notorious, for his short, witty, often biting, off-the-cuff utterances in the middle and at the end of concerts, agreed to speak in the Union on the motion that 'This house would like to appoint a dictator' – with himself in view. Alas! On the day on which he was due to come down to Oxford, I got a telegram saying that he was unable to appear; a feature of his activities which was becoming all too characteristic at that time. I fear that he lost his nerve. The same thing happened a fortnight later with Charles Laughton, who at the last moment could not bring himself to propose that 'This house prefers the poet to the pub.'

I was now nearing the end of my time at the university and I had to decide what I wanted to do. I sought the wise advice of Sir Hugh Allen, in addition to that of my tutors at Balliol. When I put the question to him, he paused for a few moments, obviously weighing up in his mind the various factors involved; then he spoke. 'Well,' he said, 'you've been reading Modern Greats here and you will probably get a good degree. You've got a law scholarship at Gray's Inn already. You've been Chairman of the University Conservatives and President of the Union. You can obviously go to the Bar and then into politics. The alternative is to take up music professionally. You are a pianist, organist, choir trainer and conductor; if you get some musical qualification you can become a teacher, but you will find yourself ending up with a life which is full of pretty dull chores. On the other hand, if you go into politics, you will always have music as an amateur to enjoy for its own sake. If you make music your career you must become a conductor, but if you do that you must aim to get right

THE ACHARNIANS
BY ARISTOPHANES

Translated by ROBERT YELVERTON TYRRELL

DICAEOPOLIS, *an Attic Farmer*
HERALD
AMPHITHEUS, *a Demi-god*
AMBASSADOR *returned from Persia*
PSEUDARTABAS, *The Great King's Eye*
AMBASSADOR *returned from Thrace*
ODOMANTIAN TROOPS
CHORUS OF OLD ACHARNIANS
CEPHISOPHON, *servant to Euripides*
EURIPIDES
LAMACHUS
A MEGARIAN
HIS TWO DAUGHTERS
NICARCHUS, *an Informer*
A BOEOTIAN
SERVANT TO LAMACHUS
A PEASANT
ATTENDANTS, DANCING GIRLS

THE SCENE

is first in the ASSEMBLY, *but changes imperceptibly to* A PLACE BEFORE
THE HOUSES OF DICAEOPOLIS, LAMACHUS, AND EURIPIDES

There will be an interval of FIVE MINUTES *after the Parabasis*

Music by E. R. G. HEATH *and* W. W. ROSTOW
The play produced by H. L. JENKYNS

to the top.' Then he added, 'All I can say about that is that if you want to go right to the top you must be prepared to be a four-letter man like —' (naming probably the best known conductor of the last fifty years). As I didn't want any unpleasantness, I decided to go to the Bar, with the hope afterwards of going into politics.

In that glorious summer of 1939 most of us at Oxford knew that a war was coming, but we did not allow the threat to spoil that summer. In fact, in some ways it made it more intensely enjoyable. One Sunday morning in May, I drove up to London with Madron Seligman, a descendant of the American composer Edward MacDowell, and two girls. In the glorious sunshine we picnicked by the side of the road and then went on to Queen's Hall. There Toscanini conducted the BBC Orchestra and choir in the Beethoven *Missa Solemnis*. It was a magnificent performance, hard, driving and precise but with a lovely tenderness in the Benedictus before the return to the anguishing '*Dona nobis pacem*'. At the end there was utter silence. Inside the hall the choir called for peace. In the world outside they were preparing for war.

Programme of The Acharnians, for which Walt Rostow and I wrote the music

3 Carols and Carolling

At Oxford I discovered a new and distinctive musical occasion: the town carol concert. At the end of my first term, like most undergraduates, I returned home, but friends with whom I had often had tea on Sunday afternoons at Headington, just outside the city, told me about the Oxford concert and gave me a programme. It appeared that every year, on the Sunday before Christmas, every citizen who could possibly do so packed into the town hall, headed by the mayor, aldermen and councillors. There they found a section of the Bach Choir, together with the Oxford orchestra, consisting mostly of local residents, under the baton of Sir Hugh Allen. The object was for town and gown to join together at Christmastide to sing carols; the Christmas section of Handel's *Messiah* and part of Bach's *Christmas Oratorio* were also performed. But Sir Hugh Allen wanted more than that. He wanted the carols to be well sung, to be chosen from a much wider range than those heard on the doorstep, and the audience had to take part in the singing. But even that was not enough. He wanted the audience to learn new carols, and for this purpose the programme contained not only the words but also the melodic line of those he proposed to teach them. And, rather daringly, so the story had it, he would from time to time ask the mayor, councillors and aldermen to rise and sing a verse on their own. From everything I heard I could tell that this town carol concert was a considerable success and greatly valued by Oxford people. I was very much attracted by the idea and I resolved that next Christmas I would go home and do likewise.

When next autumn came, I wrote to the chairman of the Broadstairs and St Peter's Urban District Council, representing a population one tenth of the city of Oxford, setting out my proposal and asking if he and his colleagues would sponsor a town carol concert. Carefully omitting any suggestion that he and his fellow councillors might be required to sing a verse on their own, I emphasized that an act of this kind by the community would only be meaningful if it were done under his auspices. In due course I received a letter from the town clerk welcoming the idea and saying that the chairman of the council would not only allow me to describe this as a town carol concert under the council's sponsorship but that they would also give it their personal support by appearing at the concert itself on the Sunday before Christmas. As a young undergraduate I had rather taken all this for granted, but in retrospect I think it was a rather more daring project for me to have undertaken than for Sir Hugh Allen, a professor of music in the university.

Having embarked on this concert, I realized that it would require a good deal of organization. On the musical side I drew unashamedly on Oxford's experience; for the rest I managed to persuade the officers in the town council to co-operate by providing many of the facilities required. Fortunately, I also had an instrument to hand to take the place of the Oxford Bach Choir

'Shared joy at Christmas'

Beginning 'The twelve days of Christmas', Broadstairs Carol Concert, 1963. My father is sitting in the front on the right, and beside him is my stepmother

and Orchestra. This was 'Our Carol Party', together with an orchestra composed of local musicians who played together for their own enjoyment under the leadership of the sister of one of my school friends.

Our Carol Party had been formed in 1923, partly with the same aim as Sir Hugh's Oxford carollers, namely to show what carols were like when they were well sung. At the same time Our Carol Party wanted to raise money to provide a better Christmas for those in need. Not only did we have in Broadstairs at that time a considerable number of private preparatory schools, twelve or fourteen of them, we also had a smaller number of homes for sick children, from London and other big cities, some convalescing from a variety of children's illnesses including tuberculosis, others coming from broken homes or with parents who were not prepared to look after them properly. In 1926 I was invited to join this party of men and women, no doubt because as a chorister I could usefully fill in the treble solos, particularly the page in 'Good King Wenceslas'.

Joining Our Carol Party opened up a new vista for me, in terms of both carols and carollers. Here were carols we had never heard of, let alone sung in a Christmas carol service, at St Peter's-in-Thanet; some were French, some were German, some were English collected from the countryside, others were harmonizations of tunes already known to me. What was most striking was the precision, the rhythm and the polish with which they were sung. What is more, they were all unaccompanied, even when we were invited to sing indoors. The party would never dream of allowing itself to be accompanied on a piano or any other instrument. All this made the singing much more interesting.

As for the carollers, from them I learned two things. First, that when we were singing we concentrated entirely on the quality of our sound. No matter how bitterly the winds blew on the North Foreland, or the snow drifted down around our ears, it was the standard of the performance which mattered. No matter how warm the hospitality inside someone's home, we must never allow ourselves to be distracted from the self-imposed task of producing a beautiful performance. But, and this was the second point, in between the music we could, and did, thoroughly enjoy ourselves. That was what made it all such fun.

By the time I joined the party, it had not only built up its impressive repertoire, it had already established many of its traditions. Rehearsals always began in October, once a week, usually on Sunday evenings after church or chapel. The party was not tied to either and members came from all denominations; some, I suspect, from none. At the beginning of December we visited the preparatory schools, one or two each night, before they had their evening meal. These occasions required a programme of five or six carols, some of which the boys and girls were invited to choose and then to join in. After this we began to

Many nights on the windswept, snow-driven North Foreland I sang the words of the page: 'Fails my heart, I know not how, I can go no longer.'

X. 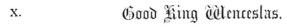 Good King Wenceslas.

Good King Wen - ces - las look'd out, On the Feast of Ste - phen,

sing on a carefully prepared tour of the main streets of the town. Here torches and collecting boxes became necessary. As we got nearer to Christmas, a small coach was chartered for each of three evenings to take us to the more outlying districts. We were just able to pack the two dozen or so members of the party into it. This enabled us to sing at the large individual houses at Kingsgate and the North Foreland to the east of Broadstairs, and at Dumpton Gap to the west. Here hospitality was lavishly dispensed, for many had benefited from the boom after the First World War. Indeed, so well fed and watered were some of the tenors and basses by the time they had finished an evening round that, spurning the inside of the coach, they travelled home in great hilarity on the roof.

Musically, too, there were by now well-known traditions. We always started the evening with the old French carol entitled 'When the crimson sun had set'. This was popularly known as the 'opening chorus'. We have since adopted a rather more sophisticated arrangement of this tune taken from the *Oxford*

Victorian engraving of Christmas carollers, the caption to which reads: 'On Christmas Eve it is still the custom in some places for the villagers and their children to go round to the best houses and sing a few of the old carols. They are often accompanied by a band of musicians, and on a clear, still winter's night the sound of this rural minstrelsy is as beautiful in its way as an anthem in a great cathedral. At Christmas-time, above all other seasons, we should have kind hearts, and give to the poor all we can afford to spare.'

Carol Book, where it appears with the word 'Angels from the realms of glory'. We always finished the evening with '*Adeste Fideles*' ('O come all ye faithful'). In between we sang a number which were new to me, 'A virgin unspotted', two versions of which appear in the *Oxford Carol Book*, and 'How far is it to Bethlehem?' a piece with which I never much found myself in sympathy. We also included in our folder, in which the carols were carefully pasted so that a torch could be shone upon them, old favourites such as 'The first Nowell', 'Good King Wenceslas', 'Here we come a-wassailing' and 'While shepherds watched their flocks by night'. When we invited someone to choose a carol it almost invariably turned out to be one of these, although quite often they asked for 'Hark! the herald angels sing' or 'Once in royal David's city', neither of which – for some reason unknown to me – appeared in our books. Sensing what the individual requests would be, we usually took the opportunity of singing one of the more esoteric carols to begin with, in part to please ourselves, in part to relieve the tedium, in part to try to persuade people that there were carols other than the old stalwarts which were well worth hearing.

Our carols finished on Christmas Eve with visits to a few big houses and the three or four large hotels which then existed on our part of the coast. We always broke off at 10.30 p.m. in order that the sopranos and altos could put on long dresses and the gentlemen dinner jackets with black ties. This meant the coach doing a round tour to drop the members of the party at their homes and then repeating the tour to pick them up again before going on to the final rendezvous at Kingsgate Castle. There on arrival we always found a party in the ballroom in full swing and at midnight the lights were lowered, everything was hushed and to the flames of the flickering candles we sang in Christmas Day. On these occasions '*Adeste Fideles*' came first; there was not much point in singing 'Christians awake! Salute the happy morn', for it was only too obvious that the party was only waiting for us to finish before they resumed their jollifications. That was always the occasion when we looked forward to collecting the largest sum for our charity from those who were in the Christmas mood and not always too clear how much they were donating to the collecting plate carried by the charming girl with the red cloak over her dress – for by now we had abandoned the secrecy of the box and determinedly exposed to public view the generosity, or lack of it, of those contributing. That over, we too were regaled with our first meal of Christmas and then, tired but happy and conscious of three weeks' carol singing well done, we went off to bed.

Our last task took place on Christmas afternoon. The money had gradually been mounting up; two or three days before Christmas the treasurer was usually able to judge what our total collection for the year would be. This would then be divided into two. Half was kept to allow all the children in the homes to go on a special summer outing of their own choosing. The other was to be used for Christmas presents for them which they would not otherwise receive from any other source. Perhaps because when I first joined my age was roughly that of many of the children who would be receiving presents, I was inveigled into going on the shopping expeditions to buy these presents. It was fun enough when one's parents gave one a choice but to be asked to join in a shopping expedition to buy gifts for over a hundred children was exciting indeed. When they had all been bought, they had to be sorted and labelled and got ready for dispersal on Christmas Day. After Christmas dinner they were loaded into the cars and we set off on a tour of all the homes, which lasted until early Christmas evening. Perhaps in many ways this was the most satisfying part of our Christmas activities. It was a tradition we managed to keep up until the beginning of the Second World War and for nearly fifteen years I spent every Christmas afternoon in this way.

BOHEMIA
BROADSTAIRS
Sunday, Dec. 20th, 1936
AT 3 P.M.
UNDER THE PATRONAGE OF THE BROADSTAIRS AND ST. PETERS URBAN DISTRICT COUNCIL
The Town Concert
OF
Christmas
CAROLS
(Organized by "Our Carol Party")
for
PEOPLE, CHOIR AND ORCHESTRA
Conductor: E. R. G. HEATH
Admission will be free, but seats may be reserved by the purchase of a Programme, price 1/- from members of "OUR CAROL PARTY," or from LANES LIBRARY.
There will be a
SILVER COLLECTION IN AID OF
THE CHILDREN'S CONVALESCENT HOMES AND
ORPHANAGES OF THE TOWN
LANES PRINTING WORKS, BROADSTAIRS.

When I started conducting the mixed voice choir, I was also asked to take over responsibility for the musical side of Our Carol Party. After the council had endorsed my proposal for a town carol concert I set about enlarging the carol party to provide the choir for this event. As a result of approaching all the other choirs in the town, we augmented the party to sixty people. Then we began rehearsals, not only in the carols but in the other items required for the concert. At the same time we had the task of getting parts for the orchestra, which agreed to play for us. The only hall available was one used for a concert party in the summer; the hall went under the romantic and somewhat unsuitable name of 'Bohemia'. It seated around 1,000 people, but it was far from good acoustically. When the Broadstairs Choral Society used it they erected a stand to take the complete choir at the back of the hall and reversed the seats for the audience. We did not have the resources to do this, since everything we collected was needed for charity, so we had to use the stage. It was difficult for tenors and basses at the back of the choir to project their voices through to the audience, but we had no choice.

That first concert was a remarkable success. True to their word the chairman and the members of the council, with their families, duly appeared and sat in the front row. The hall was packed. No charge was made for admission but people could only enter if they bought a programme. This ensured that they would have the words from which to sing and, more important, would be able to learn some new carols, for I was determined to carry out that part of the project as well. We included the Christmas music from the *Messiah* as well as a variety of carols new and old. We started with 'The first Nowell', which has remained a tradition to this day. When it came to teaching the audience a new carol, we thought we had better start with the unison piece 'Unto us a boy is born'. This also gave the women and the men the opportunity of singing verses separately. It meant my doing a great deal of vocal work to show them how the melodic line developed and to do so in a way which would imprint its changing shape on their memory. At last, with some apprehension, I suggested that the chairman and members of the council should sing one of the verses of 'God rest you merry gentlemen' alone. Taken by surprise and too disorganized to resist, they succumbed. The result was far from impressive and I have never tried it since! Halfway through the programme we had a short interval for an appeal for the children in our convalescent homes and we brought the second half of the concert to a conclusion with 'Adeste Fideles'. Everyone went home feeling rather better towards their neighbours, and the town – to judge from the reports in the local press – was thoroughly pleased with this new venture. This is how the Broadstairs Town Carol Concerts began. They have continued without a break except for the years of the Second World War and this year, 1976, is their fortieth anniversary.

The poster advertising our first Town Carol Concert

As the years have gone by, we have consistently added to our repertoire until now it contains some sixty carols. At our concert we sing twenty-four, of which nine or ten are also sung by the audience. Of course, some of the favourites are indispensable, but we are still able to work the changes year by year. The audience is never happy unless it has the opportunity of singing 'The first Nowell', 'Once in royal David's city', 'While shepherds watched their flocks by night' and 'Adeste Fideles'. Other works have also become traditional, and the more they are sung and the more popular they become, the more difficult it is to leave them out of the programme without causing disappointment. Everyone expects to have an opportunity of singing 'The twelve days of Christmas', after first having been reminded by me vocally of the tricky pieces in the score. This has been going on for a quarter of a century! There are others, sung by the choir and soloists, which have also accumulated their own special characteristics. The Christmas Day carol from Queen's College, Oxford, sung in a mixture of English and dog Latin, 'The boar's head in hand bear I' we always sing with the soloist and quartet in procession, academically clad, preceded by the chef bearing the boar's head, with an apprentice boy in front of him carrying the carving knife and fork. For many years now we have been fortunate in having the solo sung by a Latin scholar, a former Dean of Trinity, Oxford, and now Professor of Latin at another university, who, should the procession take longer than the carol allows, contributes additional verses as the procession winds its way round the hall. Over the last decade, 'We wish you a merry Christmas', always sung as the last carol before 'Adeste Fideles', has become immensely popular. This, too, has now attracted its own piece of theatre with the choir adamantly declaring 'We won't go. We won't go' until finally the figgy pudding they are demanding is produced and placed before them. Building up a programme for a carol concert like this is an art in itself. There has to be a balance between the well-known and the lesser-known, between the boisterous and the reflective, and for the choir there has to be the contrast between the different keys as the programme moves along. There must always be one or two especially for the children, like 'Away in a manger' or 'Sleep holy babe' or 'Rocking' and there must always be one or two new ones which this particular audience will not have heard before.

One approach which always gives me intense pleasure is to compare the different arrangements of words and tunes which have been created over the last 400 years. The old German chorale for 'In Dulci Jubilo' we can sing in its original simple harmonization, but there is also the Novello arrangement under the title 'Good Christian men rejoice', so phrased that it is almost always murdered to 'Good Christian men re-joi-i-oice'. There is a glorious arrangement for four-part choir and quartet of soloists by Robert de Pearsall, but by far the most splendid is the magnifi-

60

Bringing in the boar's head at Queen's College, Oxford

cent harmonization by Johann Sebastian Bach. It is to this that we always sing the last verse '*Ubi sunt gaudia*'. It is Bach's running counterpoint which truly expresses the great joy of this carol. Another comparison might be made between the original tune for 'While shepherds watched their flocks by night' in the *Oxford Carol Book*, a lively, chirpy English folk tune, and that which is commonly sung on the doorsteps. To my mind the former is an infinitely better tune but with no chance of ever replacing its rival in common use. To expect it to do so would be just as unrealistic as the opinion expressed by the editor of the *Oxford Carol Book* that 'Good King Wenceslas' should be abandoned as a Christmas carol and the original words of the 'Flower Carol' sung instead. Yet another interesting duo deserves mention: the Czechoslovakian tune used for that simple, quiet carol 'Rocking' is also sung at double the speed for the 'Sleigh Bell Carol', though very few people recognize the tune as the same for both.

What has given me greatest pleasure is to have carols especially written for the Town Carol Concert. The first of these was a setting by Richard Rodney Bennett of Robert Herrick's words of 1647, 'What sweeter music can we bring than a carol for to sing' which we sang in the concert at Christmas 1968. Richard Rodney Bennett is one of the foremost of our young composers, already well established and recognized for this craftsmanship and flair in a wide range of compositions including orchestral music, opera, concertos, works for small combinations of instruments and, following the excellent examples of William Walton and Arthur Bliss, in film music. What is perhaps less publicly appreciated is that he is also a pianist of brilliant technique. It was natural that I should go first to Richard Rodney Bennett because of his family's connection with Our Carol Party. His aunt, Miss Elizabeth Bennett, was one of the first supporters of the carollers. For many years she sang with us and still maintains her interest even though she is now well into her eighties and living away from Broadstairs. Her brother Rodney Bennett, a writer, used to stay with her and it was in her house that I first met the young Richard Rodney Bennett, admired his technique and heard some of his early compositions. One of the rewards the choir received each year for its efforts was a party given by Miss Bennett at her home, Castlemere, in January when all the work was over. In those early years this was also very much a family affair, in which we not only enjoyed her splendid hospitality but entertained ourselves musically by both singing and playing. The event which most lingers in my mind was when the actor Henry Ainley happened to be staying there at the same time and joined our party. He insisted on making his own contribution, and in a resonant voice read part of *A Christmas Carol* by Charles Dickens. This was particularly appropriate in the town Charles Dickens himself described as 'that agreeable watering place', where he spent so much of his time and wrote so many of his books.

Richard Rodney Bennett's carol, though not easy for a choir such as ours to sing, was a work of great beauty and immensely appealing to the audience. Another carol was written for us by Timothy Salter, less well known but already with two recordings to his credit. Another good pianist, he has specialized particularly in playing in chamber music groups. His carol is technically more difficult and very effective.

We have also been helped by other musicians who have come to the concert, sometimes to make the appeal for funds halfway through. When Sir Malcolm Sargent came he was, as ever, urbane, stimulating and witty in his comments. The audience loved it and the financial result was a record. But later, on the way back to London with some of our friends, he felt unwell and on arrival at his home he was rushed to hospital. It was, alas, the onset of the illness which was soon to prove fatal. I like to remember him full of fun and jollity, completely at ease singing carols with a local choir in a small seaside town, rather than as the stricken figure who just managed to appear to bid his farewell at the final night of the Proms. For the last twenty years of his life,

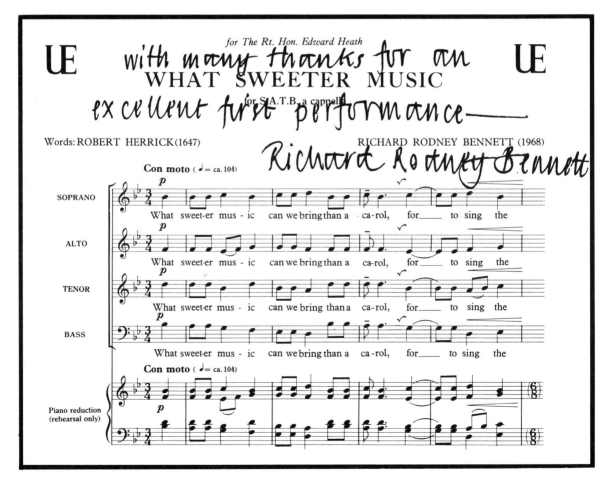

Malcolm Sargent was probably the British conductor and musician best known to the public, particularly to the promenaders, who adored him. In the world of professional music he was rather more controversial and there were always those ready to sneer. Perhaps as a result of his restless, nervous energy, he did conduct too many concerts a year; perhaps his repertoire of major works was somewhat limited; perhaps he did lack sympathy with the avant-garde products of contemporary music festivals; and perhaps he was snobbish in his approach to the non-musical world. For all that, he did a great deal to encourage British music and British musicians. He himself had the kind of grounding in church music I mentioned earlier. He was a pianist who had had to establish himself and earn his living as an organist and choir master before leaping into prominence when he was chosen by Henry Wood to conduct one of his, Sargent's, own work *On a Windy Day* at one of the earlier Proms. I always felt that Malcolm Sargent was happiest when conducting large choral works, such as William Walton's *Belshazzar's Feast*, of which he gave the first performance, or Edward Elgar's *Dream of Gerontius*. After making

the appeal at the Town Carol Concert he wrote to me: 'Dear Ted, This is a quick "thank you" for a very happy day. You gave me a very happy luncheon and tea-party and I thoroughly enjoyed the concert. Your leadership was efficient, musical, persuasive and amusing – an ideal mixture for such occasions. All good wishes, Yours ever, Malcolm.' Perhaps because of his own early struggles, he always showed great kindness to others and readily supported causes in aid of musicians and others.

One such occasion was in 1961 at St James's Palace, where he joined with Yehudi Menuhin and Maria Callas in a charity concert which I attended. It was not without its incidents. Madame Callas, having agreed to sing, suddenly decided she would not do so unless the Queen were present. Malcolm Sargent's diplomatic skills were exercised to the utmost to persuade her to change her mind, but to no avail. Finally he played his last card. 'Do you know, my dear,' he said, 'the Queen Mother is going to be present and that in itself is a very great honour. If the Queen were to come she is, of course, younger than you and a most beautiful woman. People might be tempted to make comparisons.' At this Maria Callas capitulated. Alas, on the night she arrived with a very heavy cold. She gamely struggled through her arias, accompanied by Malcolm Sargent, but we did not hear the full glory of what was still then a lovely voice. Yehudi Menuhin and Malcolm Sargent together played first the Beethoven 'Kreutzer' Sonata which happily chortled on its way and then they settled down to finish the concert with the 'César Franck' Sonata, somewhat to the dismay, as I already knew, of Yehudi. His apprehension turned out to be fully justified and in the last movement it was only with the greatest difficulty that Malcolm Sargent managed to maintain the tempo and combine with Menuhin. My embarrassment was acute, for I had agreed, very reluctantly, to write a review of the concert for the *Sunday Times*. Its compilation caused me considerable difficulty but when it appeared I found I had managed not to cause too great offence to those who had taken part.

This episode also taught me something about the finances of journalism. I paid my twenty pounds for a ticket for the concert – something which I have never done either before or since – and, having received a fee from the *Sunday Times* for my 1,250 words, I contributed this to the charity concert, only to find later that I was liable for income tax on the amount I had given away! That, for me, was an expensive evening.

Above all, Malcom Sargent was a superb popularizer of musical ideas. He played a prominent part in the early days of the Robert Mayer concerts for children and I doubt if there has ever been anybody like him for holding the attention of children when talking about pieces of music. He was just as effective on radio and television in explaining what a composer was trying to do, how the orchestra was involved in performing it and what he as

With Maria Callas at a party given by EMI to celebrate its seventy-fifth anniversary

Far right: Yehudi Menuhin with one of his young pupils

Right: Joseph Cooper showing his portable dummy keyboard to Solomon

a conductor was attempting to produce. His simplicity and humour greatly contributed to his effectiveness.

Another popularizer of a rather different kind is Joseph Cooper, who also came down to the carol concert one Sunday afternoon to make the appeal. He took great pains beforehand to find out every detail about those we would be helping as a result of his appearance, and then demanded to know all about the audience. Finally he asked me for how long he should speak, to which I replied 'Four minutes or less and five minutes at the most'. In introducing him I recalled that I had first met him when he was organ scholar of Keble College, Oxford, and later when he was a cadet in the Royal Artillery Officer Training Unit at Shrivenham where he used to mount amusing and rather pointed revues, greatly appreciated by the cadets. He was just completing his years at Keble when I went up to Oxford; he left behind him a reputation for facility in every realm of music and in particular a capacity for enlivening the chapel services, which at that time were compulsory for Keble undergraduates, by basing his concluding voluntaries on popular themes of the day. Mention of this proved fatal – perhaps I should say inspired! Having spoken his carefully prepared words, Joseph Cooper could not then resist moving the accompanist off the piano stool and treating the audience to his greatest work, a pastiche of a Bach Prelude and Fugue, based on the well-known tune 'Today I feel so happy, so happy, so happy'. Lacking an organ pedal board on the grand piano, he substituted the equivalent of a tap dance with both feet and finally, carried away by enthusiastic recollections of his undergraduate days, brought the whole work to a shattering conclusion with both hands and both feet, having taken up some twenty minutes of our time. This met with tumultuous applause from the audience who had thoroughly enjoyed themselves. The result showed in the collection.

One of the joys of celebrating Christmas is the knowledge that right round the world people of every race and colour are doing the same thing – and doing it with carols. Moreover, at one time all those who belonged to the Roman Catholic Church knew that Christmas was being celebrated not only through the same ceremonies but in the same common language, Latin, in which so many of our carols were originally written. This in itself must have given an added depth and meaning to Christmas. Alas, this is no longer the case in the Roman Catholic Church.

I have had this feeling of shared joy at Christmastide through carols in other parts of the world far from home. In 1939, I arrived at Grand Central Station, New York, on the *20th Century* train from Chicago on the morning of Christmas Eve. As a former president of the Oxford Union, I had been carrying out a debating tour of twenty-five American universities while awaiting my call-up for the Royal Artillery. I had left England blacked out; rationing had been introduced and there was a general atmosphere of dreariness and gloom. That morning, in the square of the Rockefeller Center, all was gaiety and light. The snow was sparkling in the sunshine and young skaters in brightly coloured garb were performing on the rink to the music of Waldteufel and Strauss. Christmas trees were lit up around the square and in the intervals between skating we all sang carols together. Later that evening, up on the Hudson River where I was spending Christmas with college friends, we gathered round and sang them again.

At Christmas 1944, when the Royal Artillery batteries were deployed along the Meuse, such celebrations as we had were held a day or two early because it was thought that the Germans might take advantage of the well-known British habit of sitting down to a solid Christmas dinner to cause bother. There was very little carolling going on at that time, but a year later, while stationed in Osnabruck as part of the Army of Occupation, we sang carols on Christmas Eve before going to the midnight service. Seldom has 'Silent Night, Holy Night' sounded more beautiful and we felt that perhaps the world was beginning to return to some form of sanity, despite the poverty and demoralization we saw in the destruction all around us.

It was not until 1969 that I was again away from home at Christmas. I spent it in Sydney with my crew, preparing for the ocean race from Sydney to Hobart. Despite the heat of the summer, the Australians observed Christmas with all its traditional ceremonies, but it was difficult to acclimatize myself seriously to turkey, Christmas pudding and brandy with the sun beating down on the sunbathers on the beach. The carols over the radio seemed singularly remote. In 1970, on the other hand, paying my first official visit to Washington as Prime Minister, the enormous Christmas tree in the White House, cluttered with presents at its foot for children from all over the city, and the carols sung by the American Army choir after dinner, made me feel completely at home. In my short speech, I recalled Winston Churchill's words when he had been there at Christmas in 1941: 'I cannot feel myself a stranger here in the centre and at the summit of the United States. I feel a sense of unity and fraternal association which, added to the kindliness of your welcome, convinces me that I have a right to sit at vour fireside and share your Chrismas joys.'

At least in the English speaking world, numbering many hundreds of millions of people, we can still feel that we are celebrating Christ's birthday together, in the same way and in the same tongue. I left Washington just in time to get back to Broadstairs to conduct my twenty-fifth Town Carol Concert.

Engraving by John Leech from Dickens's *A Christmas Carol*

Conducting the Polish carol 'Infant Holy' at a Broadstairs Carol Concert

4 Music in war and peace

Jazz, opera, ballet

Sir John Barbirolli rehearsing the New York Philharmonic Orchestra in the Carnegie Hall, New York, in 1936

When the Second World War came, I thought it was bound to mean the end of music for me for some time to come. But not quite. As I have already mentioned, while awaiting my call-up for the Royal Artillery, I went to the United States on a debating tour of American universities. It was thought by the Foreign Office that this might help to put the British position concerning our war objectives in a better light amongst our contemporaries in America.

When I arrived in New York at the beginning of November 1939 one of the first things I did was to go to the Carnegie Hall to hear John Barbirolli conduct the New York Philharmonic Orchestra. We had been very excited at home when Barbirolli had been chosen to succeed Toscanini, then acknowledged as the greatest conductor of the world's greatest orchestra. That night, Barbirolli began his programme with Elgar's Introduction and Allegro for Strings. New York then was an exciting place for a young man to be, always busy, perhaps hard, but with a bubbling champagne-like quality about its life; in contrast, Barbirolli brought some of the freshness and tenderness of the English countryside to the string playing of the New York Philharmonic in the Elgar work, one of the best-written pieces for strings he ever produced. There followed the Second Piano Concerto and the Overture to 'Twelfth Night' by Castelnuovo-Tedesco, neither of which have left the least imprint on my mind; but then Barbirolli squeezed all the sensuality and vitality of which he was capable from Tchaikovsky's Overture 'Romeo and Juliet'.

That was the first time I heard Barbirolli conduct. Many years later, after he became conductor of the Hallé Orchestra in Manchester, I got to know him and his wife well. There was much to admire in his performances, particularly of Brahms, Mahler and Elgar, but towards the end of his life the loving care with which he always handled a work tended at times to distort its rhythm and its structure. As a cellist himself, Barbirolli was able to obtain a deep warmth of tone from his players which became an

Carnegie Hall, scene of so many great performances

outstanding characteristic of all his orchestral work. Like Bruno Walter, he always wanted his orchestra to sing. At a concert in Manchester in his honour in the autumn of 1966 I heard him conduct the Hallé Orchestra in a rich, rhythmic reading of Brahms's Fourth Symphony. Afterwards, I proposed his health, knowing full well that he had been taken ill on a number of occasions on the podium; in fact, I marvelled that anyone who burnt up his energy so furiously could go on living at the pace he was doing. When he died, I was presented with his baton case, battered and worn after its travels over so many years. It is a treasured possession.

But America also gave me another musical opportunity: the chance to hear jazz in its natural environment. Most people seem to have an automatic belief that if your interests lie in 'classical' music you cannot be bothered with 'light' music and you will find jazz and any of its derivatives abhorrent. As a boy, however, I had been interested in any and every kind of music. When any of the well-known dance bands to whom I listened on the radio, such as Jack Payne's, Jack Hylton's or Henry Hall's, came on tour to our part of the world, I made a point of going to hear them. I thoroughly enjoyed their rhythm, their precision and their arrangements of classical jazz numbers. In their way these large bands were the symphony orchestras of jazz; today we look on them as the coelacanths of the world of dance music.

Down in the southern states of America, near Atlanta, Georgia, I heard my first Negro jazz band, its instrumentalists freely improvising as they worked the dancers up into near frenzy. In Mobile, Mississippi, I listened to small groups playing the authentic 'blues', as one would expect from a town so close to New Orleans, where I heard much more of this kind of music in the early fifties. Back in the northern states, on New Year's Eve, 1940, in Cleveland, Ohio, I listened fascinated to Gene Krupa, probably the most brilliant drummer of all time, with his band, but so absorbed was I by his performance that I found it impossible to be interested in either the party or the dancing for which he was playing.

I have an intense admiration for the rhythmic vitality and powers of improvisation of those who play this music. I wish I had had the time to study more deeply its origins and to follow more closely the developments of recent years. Constant Lambert's *Music Ho!* written in the thirties, deals wittily with the earlier periods of jazz and his work for piano and orchestra 'The Rio Grande', which I often heard played at the Proms, was obviously influenced by his study of Negro music. This has now become a specialist world of its own but I see no reason why it should remain cut off from other spheres of music. Isolated attempts have been made to bring the two worlds together, but they will only be successful when there is infinitely more comprehension by both sides of the musical language they are using.

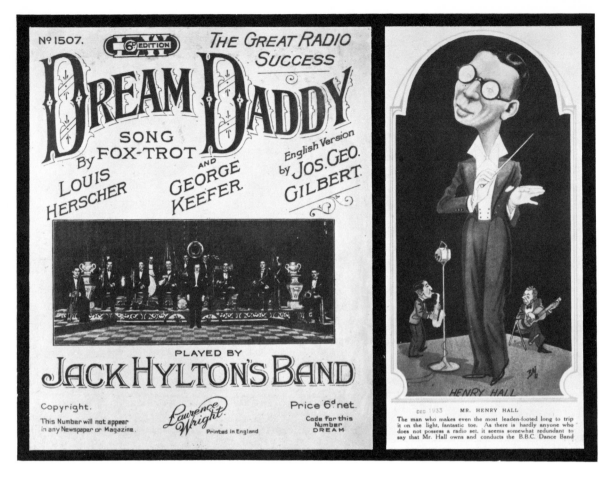

Two of the foremost bandleaders of their time, Jack Hylton (left) and Henry Hall

One figure fully deserving of respect in this context was the late Duke Ellington, who brought his band to play at a concert of sacred music in Westminster Abbey when I was Prime Minister. This was a brave attempt to play some of the music derived from Negro spirituals in a religious setting: it certainly created a different atmosphere for the enormous crowd which thronged the Abbey. But the 'Sacred Concert' especially written for the event by Duke Ellington had only been completed a few hours before, the music was under-rehearsed, and the old Maestro was already ailing. Although he came on to No. 10, he was too tired to stay for supper. Despite all that, I knew that I had spent a couple of hours in the presence of one of the great.

But to return to 1939: in Washington, D.C., on the same visit, I saw *The Hot Mikado*, a jazzed-up version of Gilbert and Sullivan's opera. Many of those who have seen *The Black Mikado* in London and elsewhere must have been under the impression that this was the first time Sullivan had been treated in this way. *The Hot Mikado* of nearly forty years ago was actually a far more original treatment of the opera. I already knew *The Mikado* well, for the D'Oyly Carte Company had brought the Gilbert and Sullivan

operas to Oxford for a three-week season each year when I was a student. *The Yeoman of the Guard* has always been my favourite. What is there in any of them to beat that entrancing quartet 'When a wooer goes a-wooing'? In fact, I was – and still am – something of a Gilbert and Sullivan purist; what I have always wanted to see is the operas performed as Sullivan intended, cleaned of the accretions of nearly a century and with their original orchestration. Malcolm Sargent did this from a musical point of view when he conducted the Company. It seems to me a mistake to think that because they are popular, so-called 'light' music, the operas can be sloppily performed without detailed adherence to the composer's wishes. True, they have proved strong enough to withstand almost any treatment, but their performance requires just as high a technical standard as that of any other kind of music. As I held these views, *The Hot Mikado* certainly came as a shock; but I was then won over by the vitality and gaiety of the performance. This, of course, was in the days before electronics had reached their present high degree of amplification, when singers were still expected to project their own voices, and when we heard the natural sound of

Duke Ellington in Westminster Abbey

Gilbert and Sullivan – scenes from *The Yeoman of the Guard* as I saw it at Oxford, and the programme cover of *The Hot Mikado*, which I saw in Washington

instruments. It is an interesting thought that the world of 'rock' music and all that has followed since would never have come about had it not been for the development of the electronic organ and the direct electronic amplification of the guitar. Without these, and particularly the latter, we should have been spared the ear-splitting noise which now so often permeates music of this kind; but, on the other hand, I doubt whether there would have been the same spur towards the exciting rhythmic developments which we have had in the last twenty-five years.

Back in England in early 1940 I was sent to a training camp at Storrington in Sussex, where I found Sir Arnold Bax ensconced in the local pub, the White Hart, for, as he said, the duration. Another trainee in the same barrack room was Robert Irving, now firmly established in New York as a conductor of ballet. Whenever we could get to the White Hart there was the chance of some talk about music with Bax – whose 'Tintagel' ranks with the best of such tone poems, even matching Mendelssohn's 'Fingal's Cave' Overture – and we shared in the music-making which went on among his many visitors. Harriet Cohen, a dedicated Bach pianist, came frequently. One Sunday afternoon they even managed to get a quartet together to play Debussy.

Once posted to my regiment, however, I found there was little to do in the musical field except to conduct a dance band. Our resources were limited, but trumpet, saxophone, piano and drums gave us a basis on which to work. We had a signature tune – 'When you're smiling, when you're smiling, the whole world smiles with you' – and we always built up to a climax with our own arrangement of 'Tiger Rag'. I doubt whether the players really needed a conductor, but we provided support for many a visiting concert party and, musically, it was fun.

Travelling around in a regiment of artillery it was impossible to carry any of my own volumes of music and there were few public concerts in the towns we were defending, though I still have a programme for one in Preston in January 1942 when the London Philharmonic Orchestra under Edric Cundell played Brahms's Variations on a Theme of Haydn – which I had played in its two piano form at school – and Beethoven's Seventh Symphony. I read with envy of those who were able to go to Myra Hess's lunchtime concerts at the National Gallery. But when I was on a short leave near London I did hear the first performance of a work which has made a lasting impression on me, Vaughan Williams's Fifth Symphony in D. The Proms still continued in the Albert Hall, despite the bombing, and on 24 June 1943 I managed to get there for the concert beginning at 7 p.m. For once there was no question of queuing; the audience was thinly scattered about the hall. A note at the bottom of the programme explained that in the event of an air-raid warning we would be told immediately. Those of us who wished could take shelter, but the concert would continue. That night, Vaughan Williams, then over seventy, conducted his own work. None of us knew what to expect. His Fourth Symphony in F Minor, which had burst upon the world in 1935 with a ferocity quite unlike any of its predecessors, had immediately been interpreted as a commentary upon the strife towards which the world was undoubtedly heading. Was the Fifth to be an evocation of the war itself, or was it to be a commentary on it in human terms, filled either with despair or with the patriotic fervour of a previous generation? Vaughan Williams mounted the platform, almost

Sketch of Sir Arnold Bax

Herrenhausen, Hanover, the Opera House of which my battery helped to restore at the end of the Second World War

stumbled his way through the orchestra, and there on the podium, bulky, slightly stooped, craggy, almost unkempt, he began the work. He had never been noted for his conducting, but the bareness and simplicity of his gestures seemed all of a piece with the nobility of the music which followed. Here was what we were searching for: spiritual refreshment at a time of strife, to remind us that the values we held dear were still what really mattered, despite what was going on outside. An air-raid warning had been given before the concert began, but all that slipped from our minds as we listened, absorbed, to this quiet, almost diffident restatement of faith. As the last movement merged into the well-known chorale 'Lasst uns Erfreuen' to which we normally sing 'All creatures of our God and King', with its recurring 'alleluias' – then hope returned to us. We were not very many that night in the Albert Hall, but we had been present at a fresh flowering of Vaughan Williams's genius.

Having taken part in the campaign through France and the Low Countries, over the Rhine and across Germany, I found myself after 'V-E' Day commanding a battery which was in charge of a prisoner-of-war camp containing a German division just outside Hanover. The job given us by the Brigade Commander was to start clearing up the débris from the bombing and then to organize the rebuilding of the city – no mean task. When he gave me these instructions he added that he had one priority: the rebuilding of the race course so that those from the Armoured Cavalry regiments could indulge in their sport. He would allow me one priority. What was mine? I replied, 'The rebuilding of the opera house'. Not the main Opera House in Hanover, for that was beyond immediate reconstruction, but a small, charming eighteenth-century building at Herrenhausen on the edge of the city. Both priorities were quickly completed, and whether our

The programme of the first opera I attended as a boy of fourteen

interests were sporting or cultural, we were able to enjoy some relaxation from the almost continuous grind of the work we were doing. The first performance I saw at Herrenhausen was the usual double bill of *Cavalleria Rusticana* and *I Pagliacci*. For some reason in those early post-war days in Germany it seemed to be easier to get to hear opera than symphonic music. Later, in Osnabruck, I heard Mozart's *Seraglio* for the first time – admittedly a rough and ready performance on a stage in a barrack concert hall, in which the night before we had been listening to a concert party and singing 'Lili Marlene'. On a visit to Göttingen I was able to hear English operas which were not in the repertoire at home, Balfe's *The Bohemian Girl* which contains the well-known soprano aria 'I dreamt that I dwelt in marble halls', and Wallace's *Maritana* which has an equally popular aria, this time for the tenor, 'Yes, let me like a soldier fall'.

My interest in opera had been aroused when as a boy of fourteen I went to Paris with a small school party. There, at l'Opéra Comique on 19 April 1931 I saw Bizet's *Carmen*. It is difficult to think of an opera more suitable for a schoolboy, tuneful and colourful, stirring and yet full of tenderness. I say my interest was aroused because I always remember a girl who sat in the tier beneath me who had continual difficulty in keeping in place the thin shoulder strap which alone held up her evening gown! I have seen *Carmen* many times since then. At the performance I saw in Barcelona, in July 1938, during my visit to Spain to observe the Civil War, many in the audience matched the cast in their colourful attire, despite the general drabness of the war outside. A horse on the stage in Act IV, however, looked distinctly underfed and rather scraggy. When the shot rang out in Act III we all automatically gripped the arms of our seats and prepared hastily to leave, then relaxed with a somewhat self-conscious laugh and settled back into our seats again.

After the war, living in London, it was to Sadler's Wells that I turned. It was cheaper than either Covent Garden or Glyndebourne, which for the time being I could not afford. At Sadler's Wells I could get to know opera in fairly intimate surroundings and at a reasonable cost, and if sometimes the productions did not match up to the highest standards this gave me an insight into the problems of putting on an opera. There, too, I was able to cut my teeth on a wide-ranging repertoire which included Johann Strauss's *Die Fledermaus*, Humperdinck's *Hansel and Gretel* at Christmas time, Verdi's *Luisa Miller* – which I have never been able to hear anywhere else – Massenet's *Werther*, Tchaikovsky's *Eugene Onegin*, and Janáček's *Katya Kabanova*.

On one occasion in 1953 I went back to Oxford for a performance of Delius's *Irmelin* at the New Theatre. I went not because I was particularly attracted by it but because I doubted – quite rightly, as it turned out – whether there would ever be a chance to hear it again. It is sad that none of Delius's operas can stand up on their own – neither *Koanga*, nor *Irmelin*, or even his *A Village Romeo and Juliet* – for there is lovely music in each of them. The radiance of 'The Walk to the Paradise Garden' from *A Village Romeo and Juliet* combines what is harmonically the most sensuous of Delius's shifting sound-textures with a sense of form which is sometimes lacking in his work overall. The suite from *Koanga* too has effective music, in its way fully comparable to his smaller pieces 'On Hearing the First Cuckoo in Spring' and 'A Summer Night on the River'. But it is still too early to form a fair assessment of Delius's larger works, orchestral and choral. Like many other composers he has passed through a period of neglect since his death, all the greater perhaps because in his lifetime his supporters were so enthusiastic and his detractors so vicious, which in his case makes it more than usually difficult to strike a balance. Personally I find 'Paris – The Song of a Great City' a powerful work; many were the times I looked out of the window of my room at the British Embassy in Paris during the European negotiations and listened to the sound of Paris; Delius's music always came back into my mind. But his *Sea Drift* and *A Mass of Life* still leave me feeling purposeless.

What is the attraction of opera? Many people feel that they would like to enjoy it but are prevented from doing so by what they see as a barrier of artificiality; they feel that opera as an art form is artificial. True, it is; but then so is every other art form, even photography. At one time we spoke of a photographic reproduction; no one today would deny that the camera puts its own interpretation, or rather the interpretation of the photographer, upon its subject. But the artificiality of other art forms is acceptable; why is it not in opera? The problem with opera is that it needs an imaginative leap from everyday life into a world in which people sing of their intentions and their emotions and do so to an orchestral accompaniment. The leap becomes even more difficult when people in part sing and in part use the spoken word.

Above: Picnicking in the grounds of Glyndebourne during the interval

Right: Carl Ebert, artistic director of Glyndebourne for twenty-five years, with John Christie in the background

Once this leap is made, however, once we accept intellectually and emotionally that in opera we are going to inhabit a world where things happen in this way, then the barrier disappears and we can share the enjoyment of some of the finest music ever written, splendid singing and good acting.

This of course is to brush aside the ever-attendant problems of poor scenery, outmoded costume, stilted production, bad lighting and foreign languages, to say nothing of singers whose voices may be well suited to their parts but whose figures leave much to be desired. In addition there is the complication of having an orchestra and conductor with lights over their music in front of the scene. Many of these problems are aspects of the quality of the performance, and the better we can make each of them the more convincing the performance will be within the artificial world of opera in which we are moving. Then, too, there is the silliness of many of the stories on which the libretti of operas are based; but many a play on the modern stage has a story which is equally remote from reality. Indeed, a story far removed from our daily lives – for example, that of Cinderella – may make it easier for us to enjoy our world of unreality.

Fortunately there has been an immense improvement in the last twenty years in its presentation; designers now produce sets which are both practical and at the same time aesthetically appropriate; as a result of modern technology producers can create almost any effect they may desire; singers now put a premium on their dramatic performances; and directors are determined to create a unity out of their work. What I still find disconcerting is that the spell is unnecessarily broken. Deep-seated, and probably unalterable, as the conventions are, I hate to hear applause for a singer interrupting the movement of the drama; I loathe to see the cast filing in front of the curtain at the end of the acts, grinning and pumping one another's hands; I dislike it equally when the mood of the last moments of the opera is immediately dispelled by the re-appearance of the cast lined up on the front of the stage. All I want to see is the curtain lift on the final setting so that we remain under the spell when we applaud.

I have enjoyed opera more often at Glyndebourne than any-where else in the world. John Christie's conception in the mid-thirties of a small opera house built on to his private home nestling in the Sussex Downs, where producers and singers could stay for six to eight weeks during the early summer with a per-manent symphony orchestra to play for them, was an imaginative and determined attempt to achieve the highest standards of both musical and dramatic presentation in opera, particularly Mozart. He succeeded, probably beyond even his wildest dreams. It was not until 1953 that I was able to afford to go there and to enjoy Mozart opera beyond compare. To drive at leisure through the lovely Sussex countryside on a Sunday afternoon, to arrive at Glyndebourne in time to stroll around the gardens, looking at the

white border and the blue border before coming to the lake, the
Downs standing out clearly against the early evening light, all
setting the mood for an opera in the intimacy of the small house
seating only some seven hundred and fifty people; and to be able
to spend the interval in picnicking in the grounds, watching the
cattle come up to the wooden fence, with all the fish jumping in the
pool, adds fun to the evening. Some people wondered whether
John Christie was right to insist on our dressing up for the occasion.
But that was the point; it was an occasion to which we, the
audience, had to contribute. We knew, too, that on a Sunday it
would not be an 'expense account' audience. Most of us had
probably been saving for some time for this special occasion and
we wanted to enjoy it to the utmost. When it was all over I would
drive slowly back to London in the last light of a summer evening,
the themes of the opera running again and again through my
head; at times I could not help humming to myself or even
bursting into song as the melodies of Mozart or the last pages of
Rosenkavalier came back to me.

Rossini's *La Cenerentola* was the first opera I saw at Glyndebourne; it was conducted by Vittorio Gui, who at that time and
for many years afterwards was the leading musical spirit there.
Carl Ebert was the producer. Names which were to become so
familiar were in the cast: Marina de Gabarain as Cenerentola,
Juan Oncina as the Prince, Sesto Bruscantini as his valet. It was a
delicious and enchanting performance; surely there could be no
better introduction to opera-going than this fairy tale, unless it
be one almost as popular each Christmas time, especially with
children, Humperdinck's *Hansel and Gretel*.

It is Glyndebourne that I have to thank also for my introduction to Richard Strauss: I saw *Ariadne auf Naxos* there the following
year. Sena Jurinac sang the all-important part of the composer
preparing the opera in the first act; Lucine Amara and Richard
Lewis were Ariadne and Bacchus, and I heard Mattiwilda Dobbs
and Geraint Evans for the first time, in smaller parts. The evening
was cloudy and rain threatened. A picnic looked unlikely and we
thought it prudent to put our hamper in the wooden hut near
where we had parked the car. As we were settling in a splendid
figure arrived to announce that he was the head scene-shifter
and that we were occupying part of his property. He did not
mind that, he said, and hoped we would enjoy the opera. When
we were eating our supper during the interval he returned. 'Did
I do well?' he asked. 'Yes,' we replied, 'We thought the scenery
looked very good indeed.' 'No, no, no,' he said rather testily, 'I
was the chap who walked across the stage at the end just before
the curtain fell.' We had to confess that we had not recognized
him. Then he added: 'The last pages of this opera are some of the
finest music which Richard Strauss ever wrote.' He was right.
Whenever I hear it, the glorious love duet between Ariadne and
Bacchus grips me until I can hardly bear to sit still in my seat. I

Continued on p. 113

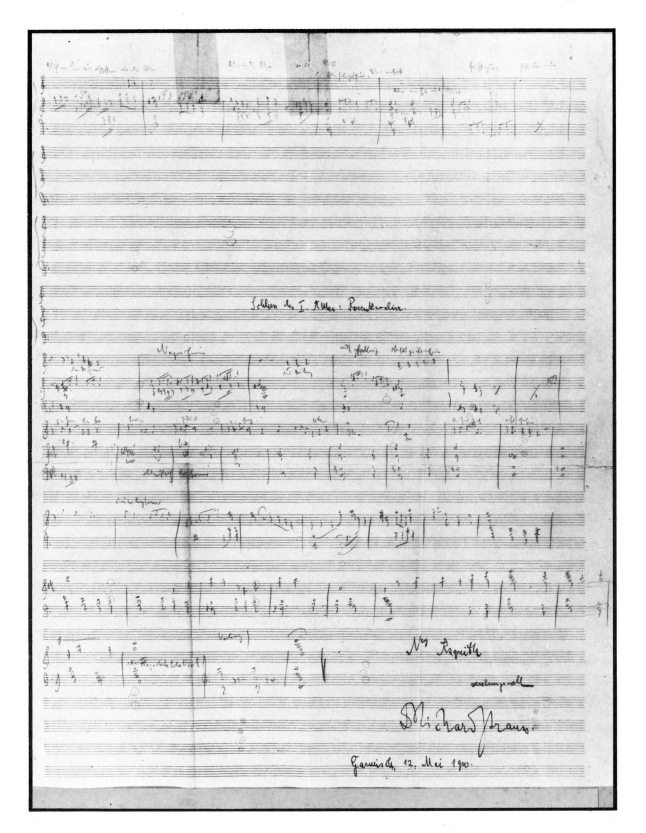

Schluss des I. Aktes: Rosenkavalier.

Nur Respekt.

verehrungsvoll

Richard Strauss

Garmisch, 12. Mai 1910.

A Celebration of Music and Musicians in colour

Mozart père & ses deux enfans.

1777.

Opposite: This watercolour by
Louis de Carmontelle, 1763, of
Leopold Mozart with his
children Wolfgang and
Maria Anna conveys the
elegance, if little of the emotion,
of the composer

Left: St Cecilia, patron saint of
music, by Orazio
Gentileschi, c.1610

Below: 'Music' by E. H. Potter.
I bought this painting for a few
pounds at a Christie's sale in
the 1950s. It has hung over
my piano ever since

Opposite above left: Johann Sebastian Bach by E. G. Houssmann, 1746. The face reveals not only Bach's concentration on the structure of his work but the steadfastness and depth of emotion which lay behind it

Opposite above right: Bust of George Frederick Handel by Louis François Roubiliac

Opposite below: Soprano score of Handel's *Messiah.* When I conducted at the Sorbonne in Paris the audience maintained the tradition begun by George II of standing for the Alleluia Chorus

Right: This painting of Ludwig von Beethoven by Elise Mahler clearly shows the intensity of Beethoven's feeling, which he expressed through the development of the sonata form. Beethoven's face later became inflicted with the agony of his deafness

The dignity of the established organist – Anton Bruckner, oil painting by Ferry Bératon, 1889

Portrait of Sergei Prokofiev, whose music for the ballet 'Romeo and Juliet' gives me more pleasure than any other modern ballet music

Right: Painting of Frédéric Chopin by Eugène Delacroix. Chopin's appeal for me is the sensitivity and feeling of his handling of the piano

Above : Programme for the concert held at the Royal Opera House on 3 January 1976 to celebrate Britain's entry into the EEC. In Europe we share the same cultural heritage

Below : Programme for the Gala Performance on 7 April 1960 at the Royal Opera House in honour of President de Gaulle's visit to Britain

Opposite: Carlo Maria Giulini, whose conducting has both intensity and control

Inset far left: The ferocious energy of Leonard Bernstein

Centre: Sir John Barbirolli, whose feeling and flexibility is in his hands

Left: Eugène Ormandy producing warm, strong tone from the Philadelphia Symphony Orchestra

Below: Sir Adrian Boult's classical poise

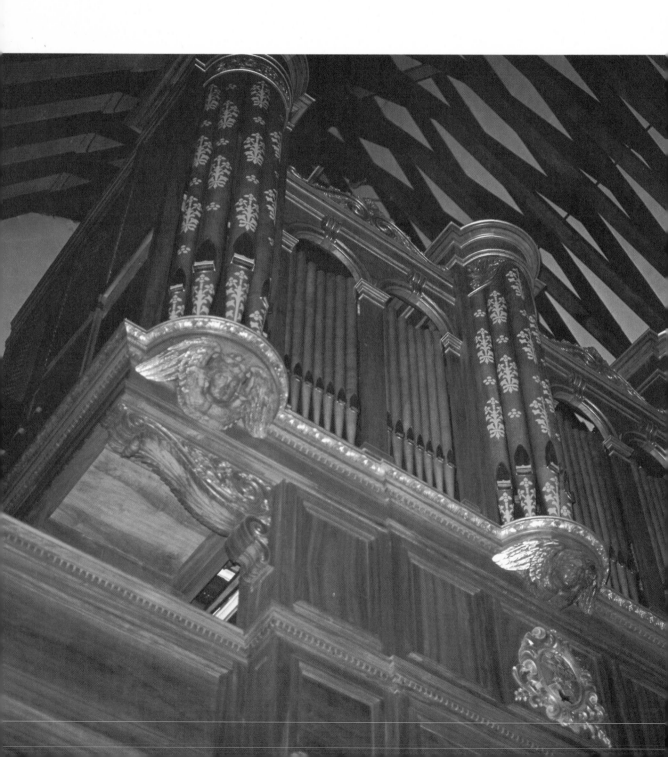

Below: The Harrison organ in
Balliol College Chapel. The
casing is as much a delight to
the eye as the organ music is
to the ear

Opposite above and below:
Playing Bach's Prelude and
Fugue in E Minor on the
Balliol organ

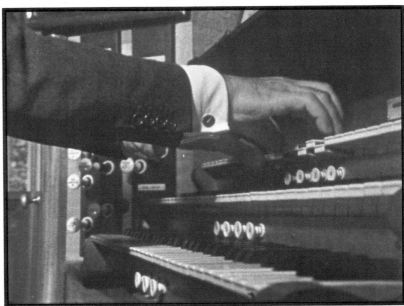

Broadstairs carol concerts in
1970 (opposite) and 1971
(above). I seldom use a baton
when I am conducting a
small choir

Opposite: King's College Choir, Cambridge

Left: Choristers of King's College under the direction of David Wilcocks

Below: The piano trio that played in my first concert at Chequers. Eugène Istomin is at the piano, Isaac Stern on the violin and Leonard Rose on the cello

Below: Hard at work rehearsing
for the LSO Gala Concert at the
Festival Hall in November 1971
Above: The night of the
concert: the full-blooded chord
before the last page of Elgar's
'Cockaigne' and (above right)
the end of a tremendous
performance by the orchestra

The Royal Ballet production of
Prokofiev's 'Romeo and Juliet'
with Margot Fonteyn and
Rudolf Nureyev. The first
post-war visit to London by the
Bolshoi was a revelation of the
standards reached by modern
ballet, an example which was
quickly followed by the Royal
Ballet at Covent Garden

Opposite: Scene from Elgar's
'Enigma Variations',
choreographed by Sir
Frederick Ashton. At first
I doubted whether the 'Enigma
Variations' could be translated
into ballet without incongruity
but it has been a great success

Above: Fonteyn and Nureyev
in the Royal Ballet production
of Constant's 'Paradise Lost',
choreographed by Roland Petit

Below: Sir Robert Helpmann and Sir Frederick Ashton playing the parts of the Ugly Sisters in the Royal Ballet production of 'Cinderella'. Helpmann and Ashton's characterizations in this field have contributed much to the success of the Royal Ballet
Opposite: The climactic scene from the same ballet

Following pages: The last scene
of the Royal Opera House 1961
production of Beethoven's
Fidelio, in which the triumph
of freedom over tyranny is
celebrated

Right and far right: Two scenes from the 1968 Royal Opera production of Mozart's *Così fan tutte*, which contains some of the composer's loveliest music

Below: The 1969 Royal Opera production of Bizet's *Carmen*, the first opera I ever saw as a boy of fourteen at the Opéra Comique in Paris

Following pages: Scene from the 1969 Royal Opera production of Wagner's *Die Meistersinger*. This is a splendid setting for the 'Prize Song', which brings the opera to its triumphant end

Above and opposite: Two
scenes from *Der Rosenkavalier*
by Richard Strauss. *Der
Rosenkavalier* is a never-ending
source of delight; it was
once described to me as a
young man's opera. I shall
go on enjoying it because it
keeps us all youthful

Above: Scene from William Walton's witty opera *The Bear* which I heard during one of its first performances at the Aldeburgh Festival

Right: *Gloriana*, composed by Benjamin Britten for the coronation, contains individual arias of great beauty, the loveliest being the lute-accompanied love song by Essex

Continued from p. 78

want to share with them the ecstasy of Strauss's music. Together
they mount the chariot, and as Strauss's swirling harmonies bring
the opera to its conclusion we see the chariot with its twinkling
lights disappear into the sky. At any rate that is how the production ended then; today the chariot advances towards the audience
– a threatening gesture. I much prefer the lovers, in my make-
believe world, to disappear among the stars. That is how I think
of them as I drive home to the tunes of some of the most wonderful
pages Richard Strauss ever wrote.

The next Strauss opera I saw at Glyndebourne was *Der
Rosenkavalier*, the opera which made him famous. Its glorious
melodies, its voluptuous orchestration, the never-flagging interest
of the libretto, all these combined with superb voices, fine acting
and an enchanting setting, exert a magic spell. *Der Rosenkavalier* has a
special significance for me, for on a music stand by my
piano is a Strauss manuscript, and on one side of the sheet is a
working sketch of the concluding bars of the first act of this opera
in Strauss's small meticulous handwriting. The notation on the
other side, which was only identified with the help of Norman
Del Mar, Strauss's biographer, is an early sketch for 'The solemn
entry of the Knights of the Order of St John' for brass and timpani,
composed in 1909. This manuscript was given to Mrs Asquith,
the wife of the Liberal Prime Minister, by Richard Strauss at
Garmisch on 12 May 1910 and inscribed by him to her. It later
passed out of the hands of the Asquith family and was presented
to me while I was Prime Minister. In response to a request from
the Strauss family, I sent a photostat of the manuscript for the
Strauss archives. I was delighted when, in return, Dr Franz and
Frau Alice Strauss sent me the original of a letter from Richard
Strauss to his wife posted from London on 23 June 1914 describing
his meeting that day with the Prime Minister, Mr Asquith. After
sixty years the connection between Richard Strauss and a British
Prime Minister had been reconstituted. These personal possessions have given me a closer link with a composer whose work,
not only his opera but also his tone poems and songs, I admire so
much.

Verdi's operas make an immediate appeal through their tunefulness. If to be able to whistle a tune after hearing it is a mark
of a good piece of music, then Verdi has succeeded better than
most. His operas are as much a vehicle for the voice as a means
of deploying a plot or revealing emotion. For me his two later
works *Otello* and *Falstaff* are the ones which dramatically and
musically give me most satisfaction. The performance of *Otello*
which stands out in my mind is one I heard in the courtyard of
the Doge's Palace in Venice in 1960. Played in the open air
against a backcloth of St Mark's and the palace, a great stone
staircase leading down into the courtyard, the opera had a
spacious and splendid setting. With Mario de Monaco as Otello,

Tito Gobbi as Iago and Marcella Pobbe as Desdemona it was magnificently sung. The scene was also very Italian. We began very late; the intervals were extraordinarily long; there were vociferous cheers after any good aria, or even a good top note, and when in the last act Emilia, Desdemona's lady, unfortunately fluffed one of her high entries a loud groan swept across the audience. It was indeed a performance to remember, but afterwards everyone quickly nipped away to the bars in St Mark's Square to chatter once again about the ordinary things of life. I doubt very much whether that dramatic performance did much to purge the souls of those present!

Falstaff I heard for the first time at Glyndebourne, where in my mind it will always be associated with Geraint Evans. What a remarkable work it is for a composer in his eighties. The physical task alone of putting notes on paper for a major opera is enormous, quite apart from the mental effort required in the conception of the work and in maintaining its structure. Those who have come to enjoy Verdi's earlier operas will at first find it impossible to believe that *Falstaff* is the creation of the same man, so closely are the threads woven, both dramatic and musical, in the tapestry it presents. It is a mistake to think that *Falstaff* relies on its stage business to make its effect, for the more often one hears it and the more closely one is able to follow it the more one sees that every stroke Verdi put on paper had its purpose in depicting the character of Falstaff and the actions of those around him.

I should like to think that in at least one sphere of musical activity we in Britain have attained standards which have been achieved nowhere else in the world; to my mind Mozart at Glyndebourne is an example of this. In 1956, the bicentennial of Mozart's birth, the Glyndebourne programme consisted of six Mozart operas, *Idomeneo, The Escape from the Seraglio, The Marriage of Figaro, Don Giovanni, Così fan tutte* and *The Magic Flute* – a glorious enterprise which has never since been repeated. As I mentioned earlier, it was above all in order to present Mozart operas that Glyndebourne came into being. And no wonder, for taken as a whole Mozart's operatic *œuvre* is unmatched by that of any other composer. In endless hours of discussion, I have never resolved the argument as to which of Mozart's operas is the greatest. Perhaps it does not matter, for each contains such lovely music, each reveals aspects of human relations with which we are all familiar, each contributes something to the enrichment of our lives whenever we hear it. *The Marriage of Figaro* has wit and style and, when well performed, a freshness which is alluring; *Don Giovanni* has strength, humour and a dramatically powerful ending; the *Seraglio* also has much humour, as well as Osmin's extraordinarily effective bass arias; while *Così fan tutte*, which Glyndebourne brought back into the world operatic repertoire, has a simplicity, charm and balance which in many ways make it the most appealing. At the tiny theatre in the Royal Palace of

Above: Geraint Evans as Falstaff, Glyndebourne 1957

Right: *Der Rosenkavalier*, Glyndebourne 1959: Left to rig foreground: Anneliese Rothenb as Sophie, Elisabeth Soderstrom Oktavian, Willy Ferenz as Fanina Regine Crespin as Marschallin

Drottningholm outside Stockholm in 1964, I saw a performance with Elizabeth Söderstrom and Kerstin Meyer in the leading roles, with the staging and costumes of Mozart's day. The orchestra too was in period dress. We in the audience sat on the wooden benches which were part of the opera house when it was built in 1766. By sheer good fortune, all these had remained unchanged in the opera house while it was used for other purposes in the intervening years. This modern restoration enabled us to enjoy *Così fan tutte* as Mozart himself would have performed it. In contrast, it is not so easy to visualize the original production of *The Magic Flute*, for this is undoubtedly the most difficult of Mozart's works to stage, and puzzling too when one tries to plumb the depths of its symbolism. But none of this detracts from the majesty of the music. Klemperer described it in his own programme note for a performance I heard at Covent Garden as 'an incomprehensible cosmic work. Everything is of the most sublime symbolism', and he then summed it all up with the words, 'It is really not a comic opera – though sometimes it seems so. Also it is not a mystery play – though it sometimes seems so. It is only *Die Zauberflöte* of W. A. Mozart. That is enough.' How, then, shall we say which of these works is the greatest? Let us be content that Mozart gave us so much to enjoy today.

Beethoven, on the other hand, left us only one opera; but his *Fidelio* is undoubtedly the greatest I have heard. Many may dispute this, but in the majesty of its conception as well as in the splendour of its music it means more to me than any other opera; and only Beethoven could have handled so compellingly its twin themes of the triumph of freedom over tyranny and of love over separation. I have seen many performances of this opera, some of them thoroughly bad, yet the spiritual content of the work always overcomes its inherent difficulties. To do *Fidelio* real justice, of course, the cast must be oustanding. There must be no weak links. Leonora must be a dramatic soprano of overpowering voice to be able to manage Beethoven's great arias; Florestan, equally, must be a tenor of high dramatic ability, especially when singing with Leonora in the prison cell in the last act.

There are some who complain that Beethoven's structure tends to break up the flow of the opera – this is very much a matter of production – and that his language is 'high-falutin'. But these defects, if defects they are, are far outweighed by the quality of the music and the drama itself. What could be more beautiful than the quartet in the first scene of the first act, perfect in its melodic line, its clarity and its balance? What more splendid than Leonora's great aria in the second scene? What more emotional than the prisoners' singing as they slowly stumble into the daylight from their dungeons, their song swelling into a great cry for freedom? And is not Leonora and Florestan's duet in the dungeon one of the great love songs of all time? True, it is the transition from this to the general rejoicing over Florestan's release which so often provides an artificial ending to the opera, and it is here that the production needs to be more spontaneous so as to bring the opera to a natural end; even so, if the purpose of an opera is to provide drama to restate the eternal values of love and freedom, with music of a stature to mark them indelibly in our hearts and minds, then Beethoven's *Fidelio* is that opera.

Having said all this, however, I would still maintain that the greatest opera *performance* I have ever seen was of *Die Meistersinger* at the Salzburg Easter Festival of 1974, conducted and directed by Herbert von Karajan. With the best cast obtainable in the world today, with the full Berlin Philharmonic Orchestra in the pit, and with a stage containing every conceivable technical device, the splendid tale of the *Meistersinger von Nürnberg* unfolded before us. The settings were admirable and the action dramatic; it was only after the performance that I learned that in the fight at the end of the second act those flinging themselves from the attics or plunging into the pool were tumblers specially imported for the purpose. The final scene was one of colour and pageantry such as I have never seen before in an opera house, not even when Verdi's *Aida* was performed by La Scala at Munich during the 1972 Olympic celebrations. With a proscenium which

The eighteenth-century theatre, scenery and costumes at Drottningholm as I saw it for the performance of Mozart's *Così fan tutte* in 1964

Maria Callas and Tito Gobbi as
I saw them in *Tosca* at the
Royal Opera House in 1964

could be narrowed or widened at will, the full width and depth
of the stage were deployed, and the grey pilasters on either side
themselves opened to display row after row of heralds. Throughout
the performance von Karajan kept a firm grip on the whole
structure and movement of the opera, and I for one found the
impact of the final, glorious Prize Song almost overwhelming.
Altogether it was a magnificent conception of the opera, superbly
executed.

The audience at Salzburg, as at Bayreuth and many of the other
major continental festivals, is drawn from all parts of Europe.
We in Britain too should be proud of our common cultural
heritage. When I returned to the Festspielhaus auditorium, just
before the third act of *Die Meistersinger*, I was touched when the
whole audience applauded, a tribute meant as a welcome to
Britain's membership of the European family as much as to me
personally. In Britain we would do well to encourage our fellow
Europeans to come to our festivals, and to ensure that each in its
own special way has an attraction to offer even the most critical of
our European friends.

There are many operatic productions of which I have said little.
In recent years we have seen a number of early seventeenth-
century operas rescued from dusty cubbyholes, reconstructed,
orchestrated, and put into production. Some of them have charm,
but I remain to be convinced that they are works of substance. It
is because most of them were ephemeral that they have remained
for so long in dusty cubbyholes.

Moving to modern times, Puccini's works are part of the staple
diet of operatic life, be it *La Bohème, Madame Butterfly, Tosca*: all
have glorious melody and excellent craftsmanship. The fact that
they are so much part of the normal repertoire may be the reason

A scene from *Peter Grimes* at
Sadler's Wells, 1963

why there is so seldom a performance which stands out. Individual
artists, yes. Maria Callas and Tito Gobbi in *Tosca* for example.
But I recall a performance of *Madame Butterfly* in San Francisco in
1953 by a Japanese opera company in which the national characteristics of the singers did not add as much to the production as
I expected. Here is a case where the recordings are more important to me than the live performances, but it is because I have
seen the works so often and know them so well that I can visualize
the scene as I listen to the records.

Benjamin Britten, more than any other modern composer, has
created his own operatic tradition and is recognized just as much
outside this country as in it. *The Turn of the Screw*, the first of his
works I saw, has left an indelible impression upon me, while *Peter
Grimes* will surely gain in appeal as it becomes more and more
widely known and as his idiom comes to be accepted. His latest
opera *Death in Venice* shows a remarkable use of instrumental
colouring in the orchestra, combined with a maximum economy
of means, but I am sure that the drama itself needs to be drastically
pruned to make its real impact. I heard one of the first performances of William Walton's *The Bear* at the Aldeburgh Festival.
This is a delightful and witty work which ought to become part
of the intimate opera repertoire. No one could say that any of these
are 'avant-garde' works. *Montezuma*, the story of Cortez and the
Aztecs in Mexico, by the American Roger Sessions, which I saw
at its first performance in Boston in the spring of 1976, certainly
is avant-garde, both in its orchestration and in its use of the voice.
It is a feast for the eye, but comprehension of the music is difficult
without studying a score. That may be another test. If you cannot
understand a work by listening to it and if it does not make its
impact on you naturally, perhaps the composer ought to think
again.

119

Festivals have long played a part in English musical life. Most of the older ones were based primarily on choral singing. The oldest, celebrating its 250th anniversary in 1977, is the Three Choirs Festival of Worcester, Gloucester and Hereford. Each year, in its setting in one of these cathedral towns, it induces an atmosphere of amiable music-making in which the cathedral organists play the leading part, the cathedral choirs sing Daily Services and the choral works are sung by amateurs who join together for this purpose, supported by one of the London or provincial orchestras. These are festivals I always enjoy, not only for the music-making but for the talk which goes on over a meal or a drink late into the night. Traditionally, there is always one of the great choral works of Bach, Mendelssohn, Elgar, Vaughan Williams, as well as those by contemporary composers such as Walton, Britten, Franz Reizenstein and Kenneth Leighton. They achieve their purpose by enabling us to enjoy and talk about music; I doubt whether they would claim to put on performances of the same standard as can only be achieved by permanent and professional choirs and orchestras.

Today, while some of the older festivals in our great cities like Leeds and Birmingham have lost their prominence, the new post-war festivals have established themselves mostly in smaller places and in a different form. Very often they have been created by an outstanding musical personality who has influenced their nature and their programmes, and around whom much of the festival revolves. This is the case with Benjamin Britten at Aldeburgh. It happened with Yehudi Menuhin at Bath and later at Windsor – and is still true of his own festival at Gstaad in Switzerland – with Sir Arthur Bliss, then Master of the Queen's Music, at Cheltenham, and with Ruth Fermoy at King's Lynn.

The one exception is Edinburgh, which provides as comprehensive a programme of music, opera, ballet and drama, together with exhibitions of paintings and other treasures, as any festival in the world. In addition, it has what in my experience is a unique feature, the Fringe activities – such as music and drama from our universities and many other groups, usually put on outside festival hours, either to provide revues and other forms of light entertainment or to give us the opportunity of seeing experimental theatre and hearing avant-garde music.

Edinburgh, as a city, with the castle in the background and its beautiful unspoilt squares, provides a venerable setting for a festival. In the eighteenth century its cultural activities were as lively as those of any city in Europe. Many of us hope that the Festival will itself help to recreate Edinburgh as a natural centre for the arts. I must confess, however, that what I have probably enjoyed more than anything at Edinburgh is being able to bring the musical establishment and the Fringe together, either at drinks or over a meal. Until I did so, in 1965, when I was Leader of the Opposition in Britain, never the twain had met. At their

Above: The peaceful Suffolk setting of the Maltings, home of the Aldeburgh Festival
Below: Peter Aston rehearsing the Northern Sinfonia Orchestra in the Maltings

first encounter they did little more than stare rather fixedly at each other, but after that it became a common experience and each side realized it had much to gain from the other. Of course, it is bound to be a rather one-sided business, for while the establishment continues in possession the Fringe changes almost year by year, and only slowly does it become absorbed into the establishment itself. Nevertheless I have always felt it a good thing that each should influence the other. At any rate, there is something for everybody at the Edinburgh Festival, and for those who want to explore music with the opportunity of seeing a play, looking at pictures or going to a show with a little light, if somewhat scurrilous, relief at the end of the day, Edinburgh is the festival with which to start.

Ballet may appeal to some as a more natural way of enjoying music and drama together than opera. The barrier of artificiality is perhaps less formidable: it is after all natural for human beings to dance to express their emotions. Perhaps, too, some trace of what occurred in olden tribal days, whether at times of planting or at harvest, whether in wooing or in marriage, whether in preparation for war or celebration for peace, whether in birth or in death, still lies deep within us: many might say that this more primitive spirit is now breaking out again in the contemporary dancing of our young people. At any rate it does seem true that we can respond more easily to ballet than to opera. The music is easier on the ear – what can be more attractive than Tchaikovsky's ballet music for 'The Sleeping Beauty' and 'The Nutcracker', or Delibes' for '*Coppélia*', or the arrangement of Chopin's pieces for '*Les Sylphides*'? And the figures are easier on the eye – what can be more satisfying than the corps de ballet moving gracefully as one in 'Giselle'? I have never become an expert on the technique of ballet, but then I have never found that necessary for my enjoyment of it. While I am sure that technical knowledge does contribute to the pleasure of those who have it, what I look for is simply beauty of movement, harmonization of music and dance, and expression of emotion and character by the dancers. When I see a performance embodying all three, it gives me deep satisfaction.

Tchaikovsky

Looking back over the post-war years two events in the dance stand out in my mind, not altogether unrelated. The first was the arrival of the musical *Oklahoma!* at Drury Lane in London in April 1947. That was a revelation. In Britain, we were still suffering from the after-effects of the war, rationed and constricted, tired and strained. That American company of dancers brought to *Oklahoma!* a vitality and colour which we had not seen for years. And when, after the final curtain, far from disappearing to their rooms, the curtain lifted again and we saw them dance each theme song off the stage, we marvelled that any group could have such dynamism and energy. Perhaps *Oklahoma!* did more than anything to show many of us what was still possible in life on the stage. The second event was the first visit of the Bolshoi Ballet from Moscow to London in 1956. Then it was Prokofiev's 'Romeo and Juliet' which we found quite staggering. Never before had I seen such beautiful dancing on the stage, such precision in the corps de ballet, such power and strength in the men and such support from the orchestra pit. That opened my eyes to what ballet could really be like. No subsequent visit of the Bolshoi has made anything like the same impact, perhaps because our own standards have risen so fast, perhaps because the Bolshoi itself appears to have lost its capacity to move forward with its productions, even though its dancing is still of a very high order. On its second visit, in 1963, it was Prokofiev's 'Lieutenant Kijé' – a big contrast to 'Romeo and Juliet' – which made its mark. The tale of a soldier

Poster of the first production of
Oklahoma! at Drury Lane

who never exists, but because of an ink blot on an official paper has to be created and eventually disposed of, is itself ludicrous; the music I find intrinsically funny. Well produced, the ballet is at times hilarious and at other moments deeply emotional, and it appears to be the nearest the Bolshoi Ballet has got to the many modern character ballets danced so well by our own Royal Ballet.

When the Bolshoi Ballet came to London for the second time I was Lord Privy Seal at the Foreign Office. On the Friday before the Monday on which they were due to open at Covent Garden, the Soviet Minister of Culture, Madame Furtseva, sent me a message saying that she had decided to accept my invitation to be present and would stay for a week. Despite this rather short notice, I was delighted to be able to entertain her and immediately prepared a programme of artistic and cultural activities to show her what the British could do. The opening night was a great success, and we went to the ballet almost every night that week. I was somewhat disconcerted to find, however, that every day the rest of her programme was being cancelled. The final blow came when my Private Secretary told me on the Wednesday evening that a messenger had arrived from Madame Furtseva to enquire about Henry Moore, whose studio in Hertfordshire she was due to visit the following day. 'Was he a modern sculptor?' he enquired; to which the inevitable answer was 'Yes'. 'Did that mean that his sculpture had holes in it?' he further enquired. The answer was clearly in the affirmative. 'In that case it would be quite improper for a Soviet Minister of Culture to pay a visit to Henry Moore's studio'; furthermore, he added, 'I think it would be better if we cancelled the arrangements for the rest of the week'.

On hearing this, I asked my Private Secretary to send a message to say that I would go to the Soviet Embassy myself on Friday morning, at 10 a.m., in order to look after the Minister of Culture personally for the day. Madame Furtseva accepted this arrangement. I took her first to the Royal College of Music, where the end of term examinations were in progress and then to the Wallace Collection. Before lunch, we called in at my flat at Albany. Madame Furtseva asked whether flats like that were provided for all Ministers and Members of Parliament. Regretfully I told her that all except three Ministers had to find their own homes and pay for them. She was astonished, but then said rather wistfully, 'In all the visits that I have made to London, this is the first time that I have been in anyone's home.' For lunch, we went to Wimbledon, saw an afternoon's play and then returned for the ballet. I felt that I had taken a firm grip on the situation and I had shown the Soviet Minister of Culture some sides of British life which she had never seen before.

That evening at Covent Garden remains in my memory, not so much because of the ballet, which I had already seen, as for the conversation Madame Furtseva and I had with some of those responsible for the production during the second act. I asked them

Margot Fonteyn and Michael
Somes dancing in 'Ondine' at
Covent Garden in 1958

when the Bolshoi would put on Stravinsky's 'Firebird' or
'Petrushka'. This led to an animated discussion as to whether
Stravinsky had now become doctrinally acceptable in the Soviet
Union. The debate ranged to and fro between the question of
Stravinsky's own attitude towards the Soviets and that of whether
the ballet music he had written before the Revolution was in fact
compatible with the cultural ideals now held by those in authority.
I listened fascinated to this ideological battle over what was to me
purely a practical question. Feeling quite inadequate to intervene,
I could only wait while those taking part came to the tentative
conclusion that provided Stravinsky meantime did not commit
any heresies it might well be possible for the Bolshoi in a few years
to start making preparations for a production of 'Petrushka'. On
that note of reconciliation we went back to our box. Views on
Stravinsky, as well as on sculpture, may well have changed over
more than a decade, but 'Petrushka' by the Bolshoi has yet to be seen.

The first performance of 'Ondine', with music by Hans Werner
Henze and danced by Margot Fonteyn and Michael Somes, was
one of the major events at the Royal Ballet during the last fifteen
years. Apart from Henze's remarkable music, whose soft surging
sound seemed to carry the ballet along, Fonteyn and Somes gave
brilliant performances. They had to, for 'Ondine' is a full-scale
work which requires the highest technical accomplishment from
its dancers. It is a pity that it is so difficult for a major work of
this kind to make a permanent home in the repertoire, as opposed

to the shorter ballet which may be combined with others without putting at risk a whole programme. Surely 'Ondine' deserves a permanent place, not only for its music but for its choreography and its setting.

The rapidly growing appreciation of music in Britain – once contemptuously known as 'the land without music' – particularly among young people, owes a great deal to radio and television, as well as to the imaginative teaching of music in our schools and universities. Television has considerable potential for popularizing music, as André Previn has so brilliantly shown; but it has to be acknowledged that in this field radio can do far more. The time available is less limited, the variety of programmes is greater and the listener can concentrate on the music itself. On radio, too, the opportunities for a commentator to explain a work are far better. In Britain we are especially fortunate in having Denis Matthews and Antony Hopkins, two very capable exponents of this difficult art. For many years I drove up from my home on the coast to the House of Commons every Monday morning. I tried to time it so that I could stop for coffee on the motorway and get back on the road again just before 10.30. I could then listen to Antony Hopkins for half an hour, week by week, talking about a composer or a work from that week's broadcasts. From him I learnt a great deal during those years, not least about Schoenberg's early works. On one occasion this proved to be a vastly expensive half hour. Hopkins spent the entire programme dilating most persuasively on Charles Ives, the American composer, little of whose work I had then heard. He played Ives's setting of the 90th Psalm, which came as a complete discovery to me. I found it profoundly moving, and when I reached London I did not even go to the House of Commons, I drove straight to the Army and Navy Stores and bought every recording of Ives's works they had in stock. I have played them many times since, but I have yet to find Ives himself quite so persuasive! Nevertheless, I shall always be grateful to Hopkins for having first led me to his setting of the 90th Psalm.

With support from the media and with financial assistance from the Arts Council, not only for the London Orchestras, Covent Garden, the National Opera Companies and the regional orchestras, but also for amateur productions of every sort, music of all kinds in Britain is flourishing as never before. It rejoices my heart in my visits round Britain on other business, very often political, to be able to take time off for a few moments of music and to find our concert halls packed. I am delighted too to find the Festival Hall on Sunday evenings so often full of young people, eager to hear new works as well as those they know well already. In years to come, they will have built up layers of memories of concerts they have heard, of those who played at them, of the disappointments they sometimes encountered, and, above all, of those unforgettable occasions when everything went right.

Nina Sorokina and Mikhail Laurovsky of the Bolshoi Ballet dancing in 'Acteon and Diana' in London in 1963

5 Music when Prime Minister

When I moved into 10 Downing Street as Prime Minister it was to become my home. I had no other. Moreover when people came there I wanted them to feel not that they were coming to an office with an official residence and a flat over it, but that they were coming to a home with an atmosphere just like their own. In my early days as a Member of Parliament I had seen No. 10 when Sir Winston and Lady Churchill lived there; in her inimitable way Lady Churchill had imbued the building with her own personality. The state rooms were not just there for official purposes; they were lived in daily and were part of the Churchills' family life. The Churchill pictures and treasures were on display in the drawing rooms. The same was true of the occupancies of Sir Anthony and Lady Eden and of Harold and Lady Dorothy Macmillan, though possibly to a lesser extent in the case of the Macmillans because Lady Dorothy so much adored the country and her garden and house in Sussex that she found it difficult to drag herself away from them.

The No. 10 staff liked to think of themselves as one family working together, and indeed, so closely were we brought into contact in this small building that it was essential for the effectiveness of our work that we should live happily together. In this we were helped by the fact that we were a small group. The Prime Minister's office at No. 10 must be one of the smallest for any head of government in the world. When I first visited the White House and found that the staff totalled over eleven hundred, I realized how tiny we were. In all, the private secretaries, the secretaries, the typists, those who looked after the Prime Minister's patronage, including honours and ecclesiastical appointments, those who answered the mail from the general public running to roughly 100,000 letters a year, those who looked after security, the telephonists, the messengers, and those who cleaned the building, added up to only eighty-three. It was difficult for anything to happen to anyone in the family without the others being affected. I too wanted to make No. 10 a real home – and for me home meant music.

One of the best-known photographs taken at the time I became Prime Minister showed my Steinway piano being moved into No. 10. After the breakdown of the first negotiations for Britain's entry into the European Community, through President de Gaulle's veto in January 1963, I had been awarded the Charlemagne prize by the city of Aachen for my work in trying to create a wider European unity. With the prize money I bought a small rosewood grand piano from Steinway's, who had recently completely renovated it. Built in 1922, it came from a vintage year – for pianos have good and bad years just like wines. Moura Lympany, the concert pianist, helped me to choose it. We toured the piano stores of London together, she playing to demonstrate every aspect of a piano's capabilities while I listened. At first I attempted to find a Bösendorfer, knowing, as I have already

'Music can triumph over the conflicts of mankind'

Moving my Steinway into
10 Downing Street, 2 July 1970

127

mentioned, Donald Tovey's insistence on this make, but they are now few and far between and I finally settled on the Steinway. It was the first time I had had a piano of my own; until then I had relied on the one bought from Thornton Bobby's, nearly forty years before, which was at my father's house at Broadstairs, or on hired instruments.

The Steinway was placed in a corner of the White Drawing Room on the first floor at the corner of No. 10 looking out over both Horse Guards Parade and St James's Park. It was the first time a piano had been permanently installed in the house since Arthur Balfour had ceased to be Prime Minister in 1906. Whenever an opportunity occurred I could easily get there for a few minutes' practice, particularly after a quick tray lunch or in the early evening after the day's meetings were over; often I would play late at night when I got back from official functions or from the House of Commons. My Principal Private Secretary once said to me that whenever they could hear the Steinway at No. 10 they all heaved a sigh of relief, knowing that for a brief time at least the demands made upon them would slacken. It was true that afterwards I would return refreshed and ready for the fray, but those interludes were beneficial for all of us.

Another instrument that played an important part in musical life at No. 10 was the clavichord in the drawing room in my flat at the top of the building. This marvellous instrument was made for me by Tom Goff, the creator also of many modern harpsichords, who not only specialized in the construction of the instrument but also executed the beautifully inlaid decorative casing. Even among musicians comparatively little is known about the clavichord. When, as I mentioned earlier, Giulini was in London to conduct the Beethoven *Missa Solemnis* in St Paul's Cathedral, he came to No. 10 so that we could talk together about the Mass for Italian television. We did so alongside the Steinway. Afterwards he said he had heard that I had some excellent stereo equipment, which he would like to hear. I took him up to the sitting room of my flat where I had it installed, and put on a record of the Amadeus Quartet playing a Haydn quartet. After listening to the first movement he said that he had never heard such pure reproduction of musical sound. I had taken great trouble over this equipment, using the best individual components I could find from different sources. In particular I had spent a considerable time listening to different makes of loudspeaker before finally settling on electrostatic ones. Even then I had had the normal wooden framework replaced with a chromium one, the speakers themselves re-covered with different material and each speaker placed on rollers for easy positioning. As Giulini said, the total effect in purity of reproduction was remarkable. Without telling him what I was doing, I put on the Sanctus from his own recording of the Verdi Requiem. He listened for a few moments and his eyes lit up and his face broke into a broad smile

Above: Playing the Steinway. The piano was bought with the Charlemagne prize I was awarded by the city of Aachen for my work in Europe

Above right: With Oscar Peterson during a recording session for his show

Below: Playing William Byrd's 'Victoria' to Dame Edith Evans' recitation of Shakespeare's 'Fear no more the heat of the sun' on the Michael Parkinson Show, November 1975

as he said excitedly 'That is *my* music.' Then he turned towards the instrument by the window and asked 'What is that?' 'My clavichord,' I replied, as I moved to open the lid. 'What is a clavichord?' he asked, to my astonishment. I reminded him that Johann Sebastian Bach had written forty-eight preludes and fugues for the 'well-tempered clavier'. This was a clavier. 'I have never seen such an instrument before,' he commented, as he gently touched the keys. The clavier is a small instrument covering only just over four octaves, roughly half the range of a piano. The strings are touched from below by pieces of metal. There is, of course, no sustaining or damping pedal. Its main limitation is perhaps its quietness, but this has its own value: when the clavichord is played, it imposes a special silence on its surroundings and induces a quite remarkable peace of mind.

The best example of this in my experience came fairly recently, when I was taking part in recording the Oscar Peterson show in a large BBC studio in London containing an audience of some 300 people. After Oscar Peterson had displayed his own virtuoso technique and we had discussed together our common interest in music, he asked me to play something on my clavichord, which had been brought down to the studio for this purpose. I had previously checked with my tuner that all was well – tuning is affected, of course, by movement as well as by the temperature and humidity of the surroundings – and I had also asked whether the amplification was satisfactory, but I had not had an opportunity to test it in the studio before the interview. Having been told that the amplification was all right, I assumed that the clavichord was being amplified for the whole studio, from which the television sound would then be taken for the audience at home. But as soon as I began to play Bach's First Prelude in C Major I realized my mistake. The amplification was going direct to the control panel and all that the studio audience was getting was the natural sound of the clavichord. Even so the instrument imposed its own silence. I could sense the intensity of this listening audience as I played and, as I found afterwards, in some extraordinary way the sound carried to everybody in that hall.

The memory of one moment at the clavichord will always remain of supreme importance to me. On Thursday, 28 October 1971, the House of Commons finished its long series of debates on Britain's proposed membership of the European Economic Community. The negotiations had been successfully settled after my meeting with President Pompidou in Paris in May of that year. At the end of the debate came the vote. We were confident of winning and I was delighted with the unexpectedly large majority of 112. This was the result of sixty-nine Members of the Opposition Labour Party defying their party's three-line whip, standing by their principles and voting with us for Britain's entry into Europe. For me it was the culmination of ten years' continuous work, argument, organization and negotiation. It was a triumph

129

The White Drawing Room at
10 Downing Street. The
Richard Strauss *Rosenkavalier*
manuscript is on the music
stand in the corner of the room

for all those who had devoted so much time and energy to the
European cause in which they so strongly believed; the opening
of a new era for Britain and for Europe. Naturally everyone
wanted to celebrate and the champagne was ready to flow. The
demands of the media for immediate appearances on radio and
television were insatiable. I felt I wanted none of these. For me
the significance of that moment was too great either for off-the-
cuff reaction or for the popping of corks. With just a few friends,
those who had been closest to me throughout all this time, I went
quietly back to No. 10 and up to my sitting room. There, as they
stood by, I played Bach's First Prelude and Fugue for the Well-
Tempered Clavier. The clavichord had its effect: after ten years
of struggle and setbacks, in success it gave us peace of mind.

The Steinway, the clavichord and the stereo were my own
personal ways of making music, but I wanted music to enter more
widely into the life of No. 10. There were many ways in which
this could be done. I began by introducing sung graces before
and after meals when I entertained official visitors. This was in the
great dining room, a splendid panelled room with seating for
some sixty to seventy guests around its horseshoe-shaped table.
Acoustically it is excellent – clear and not too resonant. The only
disadvantage of the room was one I had known ever since I first
dined there as a young member of Mr Churchill's government
at his Eve of Session Dinner in October 1951, nearly twenty years

before. The walls were hung with portraits of great men, Pitt and Fox, Nelson and Wellington, but though the sitters were great the pictures themselves were copies of an inferior kind. For twenty years, whenever I had lunched or dined in that room, I had thought how incongruous it was, when the nation possessed so many enviable treasures, that heads of government and other distinguished visitors who sat at the British Prime Minister's table should look around and see nothing but copies. In time I was able to change all this. The dark panelling was stripped and lightened, the dining room redecorated and refurnished in keeping with it and the copies on the wall replaced by four great Gainsboroughs and two Romneys, kindly lent by those sympathetic to my ideas. It was then a perfect room for music.

A group of singers led by Martin Neary, organist of St Margaret's, Westminster, the House of Commons church, would come on each occasion to sing grace and I soon asked them if they could put together a programme of madrigals and part-songs for us to listen to after dinner, while we drank our coffee and liqueurs. This they did admirably, to the great delight of our guests. They soon began picking a programme to suit each individual occasion. Martin Neary did a great deal of digging around in old folios of music, and we all had a lot of fun selecting from the results of his research. Mostly it was a case of finding words which bore some pointed relationship to the occasion in question, and when the

The dining room at No. 10 where we held our concerts. Two of the Gainsboroughs and one of the Romneys I had installed can be seen on the walls

time came we all watched to see the impact of these on our guests' faces. I well remember the reactions of Mr Whitlam, the then Prime Minister of Australia, and his wife, when unannounced the singers burst into their own arrangement of 'Waltzing Matilda'. I noticed husband and wife exchange glances across me, with raised eyebrows – 'Do these people think this is the Australian National Anthem?' I thought they might be wondering – for this was an issue of violent controversy in Australia at the time.

Perhaps the most moving of all these occasions was when I entertained at 10 Downing Street, the representatives of Northern Ireland and the Republic of Ireland who were taking part in the negotiations at Sunningdale over the establishment of the future relationship between the two countries. At the end of the first day's conference I had invited them all to dinner, but for reasons of security no one had been told where this would be, only that they would leave Sunningdale at 7 o'clock; to their surprise they soon found themselves at No. 10. There had been no gathering like it in Downing Street before. For me it was an emotional moment. I was able to bring together round the same dinner table the representatives of those who had spent so many centuries quarrelling with Britain or quarrelling with each other. Now at last a settlement seemed to be within our grasp. I was touched when John Hume and Paddy Devlin, two of the Social Democratic Labour Party representatives from Northern Ireland, came up to me and said 'We never expected to be inside No. 10 tonight. The last time we were at No. 10 we were lying on the pavement opposite in a protest demonstration and no one so much as gave us a cup of tea.' Then one of them added, 'And what's more it rained all night, so in the morning we packed it in.' I had asked Martin Neary to abandon the usual programme of madrigals and choose familiar songs which would appeal to our guests. Once the singers started there was no holding back the Irish. They immediately joined in and by the end of the evening they had taken over completely. The lilt of 'When Irish eyes are smiling' spread round the room. They went back to Sunningdale feeling better towards each other – and even perhaps towards the British.

We were also able to use the dining room for chamber music concerts. The first was a most unlikely occasion. The Amadeus Quartet played the Haydn Quartet, Opus 76 No. 1 in G Major and the Schubert Quartet in A Minor to celebrate the first issue of a new Central Statistical Office publication *Social Trends*. As Mrs Muriel Nissel, the editor of *Social Trends*, is the wife of the second violin in the Amadeus Quartet, the connection was not as tenuous as it appears at first sight. The audience was made up in part of those concerned with social developments whom we thought might be interested in music, and those known to us as musicians whom we considered might become involved in these social matters. The Quartet played beautifully, throwing off the Haydn with light-hearted zest and bringing out all the depths of feeling in the Schubert. The dining room gave them a clear bright tone. The same quartet played again for me in November 1972 at a reception I gave for the committees organizing the Fanfare for Europe, the celebrations for Britain's entry into the EEC, due to take place in January 1973, but on this occasion they played a Mozart quartet and the Schubert Quintet, a work which expressed the immense satisfaction which everybody present had, including the eight ambassadors from the Community, at the forthcoming enlargement of the European family.

Fanfare for Europe opened with a gala night at Covent Garden, a great celebration at which the Queen and other members of the royal family were present. The programme, put together by Patrick Garland and others, was composed of a mixture of music, poetry and drama, drawing on our European heritage. The main musical events, however, were the concerts in the Albert Hall. Among these one given by Herbert von Karajan and the Berlin Philharmonic Orchestra was particularly memorable. I was delighted that von Karajan had agreed to bring the Berliners for this concert – 'to please you', as he said. Their London appearance had to be sandwiched in between two long-standing engagements, the whole orchestra flying into London in the afternoon and out again the morning after the concert. Technically the evening was one of the Winter Proms; needless to say, the whole of the Albert Hall was packed, and looking at the mass of young people standing

The Amadeus Quartet who played for me at 10 Downing Street and at Chequers

in the promenade it did not seem possible to squeeze another single body in. I shall never forget the faces of the orchestra as they took their places on the platform and found themselves confronted with a typically tumultuous promenaders' welcome. Many of them gave the impression that they were hurriedly looking around for a means of making a quick getaway. Von Karajan himself was visibly stunned by his reception when he came on to conduct Beethoven's Fourth Symphony but, great extravert that he is, he responded to it and immediately established a rapport with this youthful part of his audience. Afterwards, at supper at No. 10 I learned that he had arrived with a cold, and when I asked him how much rehearsal they had had that afternoon he told me that when the orchestra assembled he had asked them to play a common chord of C and then dismissed them to get a good rest. It certainly worked. That evening produced two superb performances – the Beethoven Fourth and Fifth Symphonies. The Fourth has always been a favourite of mine, as has the Eighth. The Fourth, squeezed between the massive structures of the Third and the Fifth, is all too seldom heard, whereas the Eighth, in the same way slotted in between the Seventh and the Ninth, has always been immensely popular. Toscanini made recordings of the Fourth at different periods of his life, each one getting faster with advancing age. The reverse is the case with Klemperer's performances, which got slower towards the end of his life. I never expect to hear Beethoven's Fifth played as well as long as I live, and a tape of that night's performance is one of my treasured possessions. No doubt it was the combination of the warmth of the audience and the European significance of the event which inspired von Karajan and the Berlin Philharmonic Orchestra to the very greatest heights of interpretation and technique.

Supper after such occasions with Herbert von Karajan, whether at No. 10 or elsewhere, is always a delight, for we have sailing as well as music in common. This is why, to other guests, our conversation takes on something of the nature of a crosstalk. I usually begin by asking him about the interpretation of one of the works he has just been conducting; why, for example, has he been playing a Mozart divertimento in a dry, rather withdrawn way? 'That,' he explains, 'is because I feel that is how Mozart wanted it and that, in fact, is how they did it in his day. Did they tell me', he goes on, 'that you have now got some new and better winches on your boat? How can I get them for mine in the Mediterranean?' Having told him the answer, I then try to switch back to music again, but all ends amicably with a fairly prolonged session on each of our interests. We never talk about politics. I know of no more intellectually stimulating person with whom to discuss both the technique and the content of music. After a concert in the Festival Hall in May 1976, at which he and the Berlin Philharmonic Orchestra had given a dramatic and exciting performance of Beethoven's Eighth Symphony, followed by such

Birgit Nilsson (left) who sang Isolde in Georg Solti's farewell performance as Musical Director of Covent Garden. With Birgit Nilsson is Grace Hoffmann

Herbert von Karajan rehearsing
the Berlin Philharmonic
Orchestra

a rich, luscious weaving together in one pattern of all the varying aspects of the hero's life in Richard Strauss's '*Ein Heldenleben*' as I never believed possible, I remarked to von Karajan at supper 'I didn't see you give a single cue to anyone in the orchestra tonight to come in.' 'No,' he said, 'that is not my job. At the concert I look after the structure and movement of the work.' 'You can afford to do that,' I said; 'if someone doesn't come in, he's out – isn't that right?' He laughed. 'Well,' he said, 'they all know when they've got to come in. They don't need me to tell them.'

The opportunities for getting to concerts, opera or ballet whilst I was Prime Minister were limited, but there was some compensation for this in the variety and number of special occasions in which I was able to take part. The last night of *Tristan und Isolde* at Covent Garden on 3 July 1971, with Birgit Nilsson as Isolde, was Georg Solti's last performance there as Musical Director. At a party afterwards in the Crush Bar, I presented Georg Solti with the Honorary Knighthood of the British Empire, which had been conferred on him by the Queen. Congratulating him on his superb performance, I said that I had thought his hold on the last lingering chord of B major would never cease: the silence was awe-inspiring, so deeply was the audience involved, and it seemed

Herbert von Karajan rehearsing the Berlin Philharmonic Orchestra

minutes before the applause broke out. He looked surprised. 'I have never before met a prime minister who knew what the chord of B major was, let alone discussed it with me after the last chord of *Tristan und Isolde*,' he commented. Some years later, after dinner at his house, he asked me whether I knew which instrument was missing from that last chord. I had to confess my ignorance. 'Wagner has them all playing until that last chord,' he said, 'but then the cor anglais is missing. And do you know why? Because the cor anglais is concerned with the theme of the love potion, and by the time of the last chord it has done its work. It is no longer needed.'

The following year, in October 1972, I was present in Paris at a concert at which Georg Solti celebrated his sixtieth birthday with a concert by l'Orchestre de Paris in the Théâtre des Champs Élysées. It is not often that one goes to a symphony concert on a Saturday morning, but this was a remarkable programme, for after Mozart's Symphony No. 36 came the Berg Violin Concerto and Schoenberg's *Erwartung*. We have become accustomed to the Berg Violin Concerto and to some of Schoenberg's earlier works with their youthful zestful spirit but this long later piece for soprano and orchestra is both difficult and complex. It gave an interesting insight into Georg Solti's mind, that he should have chosen this for his sixtieth birthday celebration.

My travels as Prime Minister provided many memorable musical experiences. At the Élysée, the presidential palace in Paris, at the dinner given for me by President Pompidou after our successful negotiations for entry into the Community in May 1971, a string orchestra played Mozart's '*Eine Kleine Nachtmusik*', together with some string music by English composers, including Vaughan Williams's arrangement of 'Greensleeves'. In the Emperor's Palace in Tokyo, during my official visit to Japan, the first ever of a British prime minister, the palace musicians played Japanese music on their original instruments dating from around the sixth century. I had already listened to a concert on these instruments at the shrine at Nikko, where I had a chance of talking to the musicians and examining their instruments. The most interesting was a small pipe organ for the mouth, played like a harmonica but with the pipes actually coming up in front of the face in the shape of a pyramid. The other instruments were early types of stringed arrangements on sounding boards and various forms of percussion. The musicians at the shrine regularly meet those at the palace so that the purity of the musical tradition can be maintained free from any local variations.

In Singapore, during the Commonwealth Prime Ministers' Conference in January 1971, I entertained the Prime Ministers of Australia, New Zealand, Malaysia and Singapore on board HMS *Intrepid*. That evening we had music of a different kind. After dinner, the Royal Marines Band beat Retreat on the flight-deck. Five Prime Ministers looked down on that colourful scene: the

Sir Georg Solti, conductor of the Chicago Symphony Orchestra

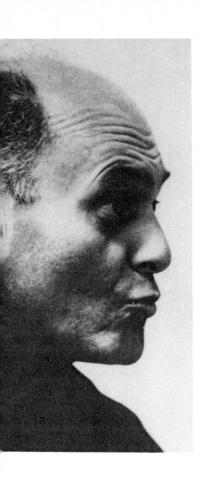

band marching up and down in their white uniforms and topees on the illuminated ship; the floodlight playing on the white ensign fluttering in the evening breeze; the dark Singaporian night blacking out the other ships in the harbour which had been part of British history for so long, but from which the Royal Navy was soon to depart. The Last Post sounded, the ensign was hauled down; we turned away. There was a tear on the face of the Australian Prime Minister.

The Navy always does things splendidly. It made me proud to be able to entertain other Prime Ministers in such a way. It was not until I returned home that I heard of one of the consequences. My Parliamentary Private Secretary told me that a slight problem had arisen over the cost of the hospitality on board *Intrepid*. 'That was an official occasion,' I told him, 'and should be properly covered as such.' 'That is not the point,' he replied. 'You see, in order to make sure that everything went all right, the Navy had a dress rehearsal of the dinner two nights before, with officers standing in for you and the other Prime Ministers.' 'Well, that's all right,' I told him. 'It was obviously necessary. We can cover that as well.' 'Yes,' he said, 'but in order to make sure everything was absolutely perfect, the Navy also had exactly the same food and wines as you were going to have. This precisely doubled the bill.' Like everything else with the Navy, a way out was found. It was worth it.

Music was introduced into the celebrations of the twenty-fifth anniversary of the creation of the United Nations, held in New York in October 1970. I was delighted that the Los Angeles Symphony Orchestra was chosen to play on this occasion. One evening, after an official dinner, wishing to get away from all the problems of international politics, I rang up Leonard Bernstein's flat to see if I could drop in for a nightcap. He and his wife were there, and when I arrived we immediately became involved in yet another international argument, this time over Vietnam, about which he felt passionately. (We never meet without talking politics.) As usual, we went on far into the night and the party only broke up when he said he must get some sleep before he went to the recording studio early that morning to play and conduct Ravel's Piano Concerto. 'I remember you playing that in London with the New York Philharmonic', I said, 'in 1963.' He ruminated. 'I had forgotten that. What else did I play?' 'The Dvořák No. 2 in D Minor,' I told him, 'and you pulled it this way and pushed it that way until its shape was entirely unrecognizable.' 'Now I remember,' he said. 'God! what a neurotic performance that must have been.'

Somehow my talks with Bernstein always seem to be late at night. One evening, after the House of Commons rose, I went down to the Albert Hall to watch him listening to the replays of the Verdi Requiem, which he had just finished recording, picking the particular ones he wanted and supervising the mix. All around were technicians, in their shirtsleeves, listening with him

to the quadraphonic sound. It was a fascinating experience. Bernstein and von Karajan seem to be in a class on their own when it comes to the technology of recording and reproducing music. On another occasion in my flat in Albany, I pressed him hard on the organization and management of orchestras. At 4 o'clock in the morning, he finally came clean and declared that a firm central authority, be it conductor or management, was essential if a symphony orchestra was not only to attain the highest standards but, what was even more difficult, maintain them over a sufficient period of time to be in the top three or four of the world class. Lennie Bernstein is one of those to whom everything in music appears to come easily: a brilliant pianist, a successful composer of both musicals and symphonic works, a masterly, if individualistic, conductor, a stimulating writer, and a popularizer of music who can hold any audience spellbound whether on television or in the concert hall. One cannot but wonder at the extraordinary fount of energy on which he draws for this activity. In addition, he feels passionately about injustice and the underprivileged, an interest he has in common with Isaac Stern and Yehudi Menuhin.

Above left: Leonard Bernstein at rehearsal

Above: Isaac Stern, who twice played for me at Chequers

Music was always provided on my official visits to the White House in Washington. In February 1972 Beverly Sills came from the Metropolitan Opera to sing. I have already mentioned my earlier visit in 1970 just before Christmas, when the American Army choir sang carols. After flying back to conduct my own carols at Broadstairs, I then returned to No. 10, where we always had carols round our own Christmas tree in the large pillared room. A group from the London Bach Choir came each year to sing to us, as friends and staff all sat around the room, many of them on the floor. On one occasion President Nixon's daughter Tricia and her husband arrived just in time to have a meal and join in. It made them feel at home.

At Chequers we always had carols on Christmas Eve. The carollers came from the local church to sing in the great hall for our Christmas party, with the tree twinkling in the corner and the other lights dimmed. It became quite a tradition and we got to know the choir well. Once, as we were all having mince pies and some winecup together, I asked one of the oldest members of the choir whether she could recall this kind of thing ever happening before. 'Yes', she replied, 'but only once under another Prime Minister. It was when Mr Ramsay MacDonald was here in 1923. But then, of course, we had to come in by the kitchen, up the stairs and on to the balcony. We weren't allowed to mix downstairs. Not even Mr MacDonald could fix that in those days.'

Chequers was presented to the British nation in 1919 by Lord Lee of Fareham to provide a country home for rest and relaxation for the British Prime Minister. It is a splendid unspoilt Tudor house containing many treasures including the State ring of Queen Elizabeth I of England, together with some of Cromwell's letters and Napoleon's letters and papers. What was originally the centre courtyard of the Tudor house has been closed in and made into the great hall, and this provides an excellent room for concerts of all kinds. There I installed a further set of stereo equipment; there was already a Steinway in the house, but for concert purposes Steinway's always lent us one of their own pianos.

Our first concert at Chequers proved more eventful than we had expected. Isaac Stern, an old friend, suggested that his trio should play a Beethoven programme for me before they started their series of concerts in London. This was arranged for 9 September 1970, during the Parliamentary recess when I hoped nothing could interfere with it. As it happened, the evening came at the height of the crisis over the hijacked aircraft with 300 or more passengers held hostage at Dawson's Field in the Jordanian desert. This also involved Leila Khaled, who had been taken off an Israeli aircraft in London and was being held by the immigration authorities. At least five countries had nationals on board the hijacked aircraft and their representatives were meeting with the International Red Cross at Geneva. Events were moving so fast, and the need for speedy decisions was so great, that it was obvious by the middle of the afternoon that I could not leave No. 10 to go down to Chequers for the concert. When the trio arrived at Chequers they were deeply worried about the possible effects of the crisis on the whole of the Middle East, and they were obviously very tense. I passed a message to them on the telephone, expressing the hope that they would continue with the concert in my absence. Despite all their worries they agreed to do so.

The tension made itself felt in Isaac Stern's playing of Beethoven's Violin Sonata in F, known as the 'Spring' Sonata, but after that it disappeared. This is apparent on the tape recording I have. Rose and Istomin played Beethoven's Cello Sonata No. 3 in A Major, Opus 69, most beautifully. The concert ended with Beethoven's 'Archduke' Trio because it was known to be my favourite. Isaac Stern said afterwards that as he was playing the Violin Sonata he realized that Beethoven's music was stronger than the anxieties and horror of the political situation: it was at just such a time that one most needed to remind oneself of the values and traditions which Beethoven represented. The other players felt the same and on that eventful night they conveyed it to the friends and neighbours gathered round them in the great hall at Chequers.

Yehudi Menuhin, another old friend, brought some of the children from his school to play in November 1970. They were young, but how assured they were. A boy of thirteen playing the cello brilliantly found the pin sliding on the floor soon after he had begun. Yehudi stopped him and we placed a rug underneath his chair so that he could get a proper grip. He was not the least put out and threw off his pyrotechnics with even greater confidence. A pianist and violinist from Singapore brought home to me how much more important a part young people from the Far East are now playing in European music-making, with many others from Japan, Korea, Hong Kong and the Philippines coming on to the scene.

Yehudi himself was not billed to play in the programme, but he had suggested that the evening might conclude with an impromptu performance by the two of us. We had decided to play the Handel Sonata in D Major. I particularly checked with him the edition he used and practised it hard beforehand. We rehearsed the piece together at Chequers before the concert began and all seemed to go well. When the children had finished their part of the concert, ending up with the first movement of the Brahms Sextet, I went up to fetch Yehudi from his room. The audience was delighted at the idea of this 'lollipop', but when we began it became obvious, to my astonishment, that Yehudi was extraordinarily nervous. In the second movement he began to play faster and faster, and I had some difficulty in keeping up with him. In the third movement we settled down, but in the last movement we began a race for the finish. Then, suddenly, I had

Sir Arthur Bliss (right) and Clifford Curzon discussing Bach

a bad moment: I realized that Yehudi was playing from memory, although he had his music open in front of him, and he was clearly playing from a different edition. Hastily looking to see what had happened, I found that he had jumped four bars ahead of me. I skipped everything to fit in with him and with a quick adjustment I made sure we finished together. Our audience appeared to have appreciated the performance; perhaps the slight sense of competition rather than partnership had heightened their enjoyment. Over supper only one music critic commented on the four missing bars.

The pianist Clifford Curzon came down to play at Chequers on Sunday, 9 July 1972, my birthday. It was a lovely summer evening. We were able to stroll around the rose garden before the concert and chat outside afterwards. Clifford Curzon told me he wanted to play one piece to please himself and one to please me. The first was the Variations on a theme from 'Prometheus' by Beethoven, probably better known to most people as it appears in the last movement of the 'Eroica' Symphony. It is a massive work, seldom played, and one which I would not have thought would appeal particularly to Curzon, but he produced an invigorating,

indeed exciting, performance which he has since recorded. After the break, he began to play me Schubert's 'Posthumous' Sonata in B Flat, surely one of the loveliest piano sonatas ever written. Pianists seem to despise Schubert's piano sonatas today, not realizing that many of them require a simplicity, clarity and sureness of technique to express without effort their underlying emotion which is available only to the very best. I first heard this sonata played by Richter at the Aldeburgh Festival one glorious June Sunday afternoon. It was pure joy. He played the first movement more slowly than anyone else I have ever heard and with the repeats journeyed on effortlessly and apparently endlessly; I never wanted it to stop. Clifford Curzon knew how I felt about it, and that night we settled back to bask anew in the freshness of what was almost Schubert's last great piano work. This work too Clifford Curzon has now recorded. Four years later, at an impromptu supper party, at my publisher's house in Paris, near the university, Paul Badura-Skoda, who has recorded all the Schubert piano sonatas, asked me what he should play. 'The B Flat "Posthumous",' I replied 'with all the repeats.' 'With *all* the repeats?' he asked, somewhat incredulously. 'Yes', I said, '*all* the repeats.' He sat down at the piano and when he got to the repeat halfway through the first movement, and played the first time bars before going back to the beginning, his wife turned to me in astonishment and said 'I have never heard those eight bars played before.' It was all part of Schubert's heavenly length. Before this, we had been listening to and applauding some Schumann – '*Papillons*' – brilliantly played by a young Cypriot pianist, Cyprien Katsaris. At the end of the Schubert no one moved. It was so deeply satisfying that no one felt the need to applaud. We rested content.

The Greek pianist Gina Bachauer, who had heard Clifford Curzon's concert at Chequers, said she would like to play for my next birthday concert on 8 July 1973. It was once again a fine evening with the sun shining and the roses in full bloom. After Gina had finished, we once again had an impromptu item – this time unknown to me. Georg Solti announced that he had brought with him a new and important recording which he wished to play on my stereo before we broke up for supper. Everyone was intrigued to know what this could be. Some of us knew that he was busy doing Mozart's *Così fan tutte* for Decca and we were all delighted when his distinguished singers burst into the sextet '*Alla bella Despinetta*' from the first act of *Così*. The point only became clear, however, when the cast, led by Lorengar, Berganza, Krause and Davies, each in their own language, and then the full company in English, sang 'Happy Birthday, Dear Ted' to the background of a harpsichord – happy birthday greetings indeed. The disc given to me afterwards bears the inscription 'Soldecca Group – Very advanced recording', with the names of the artists followed by the very modest 'accompanist G. Solti'.

The visit of Dr Caetano, the Portuguese Prime Minister, to London in July 1973, to mark the 600th anniversary of the first Anglo-Portuguese Treaty of Alliance, gave me the opportunity of commissioning a special piece of music in honour of the occasion, to be performed at my dinner for the visiting Prime Minister in the Painted Hall at Greenwich. I invited Sir Arthur Bliss, the Master of the Queen's Music, to compose a piece to be sung by the Martin Neary singers. For the words, Tom Bridges, grandson of the former Poet Laureate and one of my private secretaries, suggested an English translation of a Portuguese poem, '*Mar Português*' – 'Portuguese Sea', a subject which naturally appealed to me. Sir John Betjeman, the Poet Laureate, was invited to write the English words, and Alan Goodison of the Foreign Office was asked to translate the Portuguese into English to enable him to do so. In order to give Sir Arthur an idea of what was involved the translation was sent to him before Sir John's poem was ready; in fact, when the Poet Laureate's verses arrived, the Master of the Queen's Music found that he preferred Alan Goodison's translation for the purpose of a musical setting. In the event, we printed both Sir John Betjeman's poem and Alan Goodison's translation in the menu, together with the Portuguese original. Sir Arthur Bliss's music has since been published. It was sung in the Painted Hall by the augmented body of singers under Martin Neary, divided into two groups, one on each side at the top of the staircase leading into the hall, whose resonance greatly helped the performance. It is a splendid piece, to my mind amongst the most effective of Arthur Bliss's smaller choral works. It was certainly a piece for an occasion, and it added lustre to this one.

The concert which will be longest remembered of all those we had in Downing Street and at Chequers will be the one I gave at No. 10 to celebrate Sir William Walton's seventieth birthday on 29 March 1972. I felt that, despite the honours conferred upon him, William Walton had not always received the recognition he deserved, in particular, perhaps, from his fellow musicians. This was an opportunity to do homage to him in which many of his contemporaries could take part. I decided to mark the evening by having some new pieces composed in his honour, as well as by arranging a performance of some of his own work.

The veteran English composer Herbert Howells contributed a grace, the words written specially for the occasion in my private office. After its first performance at this dinner, the words were adapted to general use, and the grace was sung before every subsequent dinner at No. 10. Arthur Bliss wrote a witty piece to some amusing words by the poet Paul Dehn, a close friend and past collaborator with Walton, entitled 'An Ode for William Walton'. This, together with Walton's 'Set Me as a Seal upon Thine Heart', one of the latest of his small choral pieces, was sung by the Martin Neary singers. Then, as we sat round the great horseshoe table, the London Sinfonietta, conducted by David

Above: Sir William Walton at work on a score

Opposite: The grace written by Herbert Howells for the dinner at 10 Downing Street in honour of William Walton's seventieth birthday

Atherton, and with Alvar Liddell as narrator, performed ten movements from *Façade*, the precocious music to words by Edith Sitwell which first made Walton famous. It was a sparkling performance which brought back all the glitter, the fun and at the same time the hardness of the 'twenties.

After that, we moved into the large pillared drawing room. As midnight approached, I recalled to everyone there how I heard William Walton asked, in an interview on his sixtieth birthday, whether there was any piece of music he would have liked to have composed himself. Without pausing for a moment, he had replied, 'Yes, Schubert's B Flat Trio.' And so, at midnight, with the Queen Mother and the Waltons sitting on the sofa, and the rest of us, including the Blisses, Herbert Howells and Ben Britten of the older generation, Malcolm Arnold and Richard Rodney Bennett of the younger composers; Lionel Tertis, the greatest of viola players, then well over ninety, with his wife; the Soltis, Fred Ashton from the ballet, Laurence Olivier, Bryan Forbes, Nanette Newman and those whom many would term the 'Arts Establishment', Lord Clark, Arnold Goodman, Jenny Lee and the Droghedas, with many other friends, sitting around on the floor, we heard John Georgiadis and Douglas Cummings, the leader of the London Symphony Orchestra and the first cellist, together with the pianist John Lill, play the Schubert B Flat Trio. They had never played it before; in fact, they had never until then played together as a trio. But they had spent the whole of the previous weekend working on it, and they had recognized the first requisite for playing Schubert, to let him speak for himself. The performance that evening had a wonderful spontaneity and freshness about it. It recalled to my mind the days when Thibaud, Casals and Cortot, probably the most famous trio of all time, had often played it together. It was a joyful ending to a happy evening in tribute to an original and distinguished British musician.

Our last concert at Chequers while I was Prime Minister proved to be even more eventful than our first. Isaac Stern and Pinchas Zukerman were both coming to play a programme of violin duos on 27 October, the same as they were giving at the Royal Festival Hall two days later. Alas, earlier in October, the Yom Kippur War broke out and brought tensions between the Israeli and British governments. Pinchas Zukerman felt unable to play but Isaac Stern, for the sake of his friendship with me, and even though it might expose him to criticism, decided to take part. The programme had to be completely changed, but it led to the most momentous musical evening we ever had. As the Amadeus Quartet were coming as guests to Chequers, I invited them to bring their instruments with them, and they opened the concert by playing the Haydn Quartet Opus 54 No. 2, which they had been playing at the Edinburgh Festival the previous month. Isaac Stern brought down with him a videotape of Pablo Casals's last performance in Tel Aviv before he died. After Isaac Stern had described the occasion, we showed this videotape on the screen in the great hall. It was intensely moving to watch and hear the frail Casals playing with the utmost simplicity a little piece called 'The Nightingale' for unaccompanied cello. It was a lovely message to leave with the world. The atmosphere was very emotional when Isaac Stern began to play Bach's Chaconne in D Minor as his own personal tribute to Casals whom he had known so well. He had not been playing for very long when the hairs of his bow broke and he had to interrupt his playing to fetch another bow. He came back shortly afterwards, made a brief apology, and then gave an unforgettable performance of the Chaconne. My private office subsequently recovered the hairs from the broken bow, had them set in transparent plastic and presented them to me as a Christmas present. This concert showed once again how music can triumph over the conflicts and indeed the agonies of mankind.

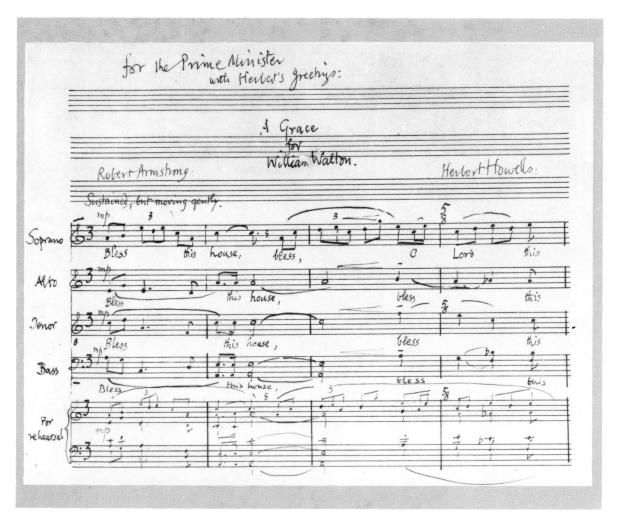

6 Conducting

'A symphony
orchestra
has a life
of its own'

We are living in the age of the large symphony orchestra and the virtuoso conductor. In the Western world in recent years an ever-increasing public has flocked to see and hear them, and the phenomenon is now repeating itself in the East. There such countries as Japan and the Philippines are building up their own orchestras, but it is the world-wide tours of the leading orchestras of Europe and the United States, playing to mass audiences in the capitals of the countries round the Pacific, Australasia and the Indian subcontinent, which have given the impetus to this. Today there are only a few instrumentalists who are able to fill the big concert halls of the world. In any case, their music is more enjoyable played in more intimate surroundings, with audiences of a few hundred people rather than a few thousand. But a symphony orchestra is big business – often on an international scale, with all the complexities and problems that that entails.

A symphony orchestra has a life of its own. More than a hundred people constantly rehearsing together, playing together and for a large part of the time travelling together, often for quite long periods abroad, get to know each other's whims and idiosyncrasies well. They size up each other's capabilities, both musically and socially speaking. It is on tour that the humorist emerges, keeping the rest entertained and relaxing the tension when things go wrong; at the same time, those who like to keep themselves to themselves quietly disappear into the background. I have had experience of this with the London Symphony Orchestra, with which I first became associated some fifteen years ago as Chairman of the Trustees. I am also an Honorary Member and occasional conductor of this fine orchestra, and when it celebrated its seventieth birthday in 1974 with a gala concert I had the privilege of conducting the opening piece, the overture from *Die Meistersinger*, the first item played by the orchestra at its first concert under Richter.

In May 1975 I travelled with the orchestra to Germany for concerts in Cologne and Bonn, where I was to conduct Elgar's 'Cockaigne' Overture, the work with which I had made my debut with the LSO in 1971 (I shall return to this event later). The orchestra had its own special plane; the fun, the ragging, the badinage on board was tremendous. André Previn, the LSO's permanent conductor, was in the midst of this; not for him the splendid isolation maintained by some conductors in an attempt to uphold their status. He was one of the boys and enjoyed it. At the rehearsal in Cologne the atmosphere was far different; there was an immediate concentration on the work in hand, not from a desire to get through the whole programme but from a need to test the hall and then to polish up those bits of the works where difficulties had previously been encountered. The concert that evening was on the whole an immense success, even though the hall was over-resonant. But one incident touched on an aspect of programme planning which at some time or another confronts every conductor with a problem of both intellectual and musical integrity.

The orchestra began by displaying its virtuosity in Berlioz's overture 'Le Corsair' – a splendid piece with which to get the audience warmed up. Then André Previn played Mozart's Piano Concerto in C Minor, K.491, a great work which in its first movement explores a wide range of emotion and in the last expresses all its joy in the Rondo; in between comes an Andante of exquisite simplicity. André Previn both played the solo part and conducted the orchestra from the piano. Although this was the original manner of performing a work of this kind, it is difficult to do so in a modern concert hall and at the same time secure the precision of orchestral playing and the kind of rapport between soloist and orchestra to which listeners have now become accustomed. The degree of understanding between André and the LSO is so great, however, that it is natural for them to make music together in this way, particularly when, as in this concerto, a rather smaller orchestra is involved. In any case it is a work which André plays most beautifully. No doubt there are some who would prefer a more robust attitude to late Mozart but his interpretation has a clarity and distinction which are very much his own.

After Elgar's 'Cockaigne' André was bringing the programme to an end with the suite from Prokofiev's music for the ballet 'Romeo and Juliet'. This is a work which the orchestra has recorded in its entirety. 'What an evening it would be,' André once said to me, 'if we could do "Romeo and Juliet" at Covent Garden, playing in the pit.' What an evening indeed! It would be comparable to the Berlin Philharmonic Orchestra playing for Die Meistersinger or Fidelio in Salzburg.

The suite itself, which the LSO has played on innumerable occasions, contains some of Prokofiev's most ravishing music, vividly illustrative and sumptuously orchestrated; I find the last few pages amongst the most absorbing in the whole of ballet music, with the haunting lovers' theme returning just before the piece concludes with the quiet, slowly dying chords of the death scene. For this concert, André told me, he had decided to alter the order of the suite so as to place the rumbustious music for the fight after the death scene. Although it would make nonsense of the chronology of the ballet, he thought it would make a better conclusion to the suite as well as to the concert, and would 'bring the audience cheering to its feet'. I sat at the back of the orchestra and listened to the performance. The concluding bars of the death scene were as full of tension as ever; the last chord died away, then all hell broke loose as the orchestra launched itself with fury into the fight. I could see that the audience were perplexed, and when the piece came to an end with the final thundering chord there was an ominous silence, followed by somewhat muted applause.

That night, after we had been to the champagne party for the orchestra – one of the few bonuses they get when I am with them – and were driving down to Bonn to stay with the British Ambassador, I looked at André and said: 'Well . . . ?' 'No,' he said rather wearily, 'it didn't come off, and all because I did it for the wrong reason.' That was the reply of a very honest man. The next night, in Bonn, he went back to the original order of the suite. Again the emotion in the last few bars was intense. So quietly were the final chords played that even after the last André was able to hold his hands still, with no sound coming from the orchestra and utter silence in the audience. Then he dropped his hands to his sides. The applause was immediate and deafening. The quiet intensity of those concluding bars had made their impact in a way in which the fight could never have done. Both Shakespeare and Prokofiev knew what they were about.

At a lunch in Bonn at which many of my musical, political and sailing friends were present, a journalist approached André. He was not a music critic, he explained, but he wanted to give the LSO a good general write-up because of the immense impact it was making on this tour. One thing, however, was worrying him; perhaps André could help with an explanation. 'Of course, if I can,' answered André. 'I am told,' said the journalist, 'that when you are conducting, both you and Mr Heath use a score. What is the explanation of that?' 'Oh, that's simple,' replied André, 'you see both Mr Heath and I have perfectly good eyesight.' This answer obviously baffled the journalist and André, taking mercy on him, added: 'You see, conducting without a score became fashionable after Toscanini. His eyesight was so poor that he could not read one on the podium. Ever since then many people have thought that to be a great conductor you need to do without a score. It's not really relevant: it's the result that matters.'

I have no doubt that those who can master and memorize a score completely have, on the whole, an advantage over others when conducting an orchestra. On the other hand, if part of their mental energy is devoted to remembering the score, rather than concentrating on what the orchestra is doing, it seems to me that they are at a disadvantage. Equally so is the conductor who has to have his head buried in the score the whole time. But the use of a score should never be held against any conductor; it can certainly be of help to have one at hand when anything goes wrong. It is the conductor who can handle a complete opera without a score who is taking the greatest risks, not only with the orchestra but with singers and chorus; perhaps he is most to be admired when he pulls it off. I once watched Karajan conduct a performance of *Die Meistersinger* at Salzburg – lasting four hours – without a score. When I went to see him in his room before the last act, he was refreshing his mind from the score, 'but only the structure, not the details,' he said. It was that

Sergei Prokofiev, composer of the ballet music 'Romeo and Juliet' and 'Lieutenant Kijé'

emphasis on the structure, that complete confidence in the orchestra, singers and chorus playing their part, which enabled him to produce a magnificent performance.

André Previn's reply to the press correspondent notwithstanding, I have seen him conduct on many occasions without a score. He himself recalls some of the hazards, however. On one American tour, the LSO were playing Beethoven's Fifth Symphony and Brahms's Fourth Symphony as two of the major items in their programme, reversing the order on alternate evenings to make some slight change and thus relieve the tedium of the tour. One night, towards the end of their visit, André waved the librarian aside, saying: 'Don't bother to put the score on tonight – I'll do without it.' He went on to the stage fully convinced they were beginning with Brahms's Fourth. After the applause which greeted him he turned to the orchestra and lifted both hands high above his head ready to bring in the drooping phrases of the opening bars. Just as he was poised for this moving moment, he heard the leader of the orchestra say clearly and firmly: 'Beethoven Five.' All he could do was drop both hands to his sides and reposition himself for the very different entry required for the opening notes of Beethoven's best-known symphony. But he had been saved.

Incidentally, I find the opening bar of Beethoven's Fifth the most controversial of any orchestral piece though I seldom hear it discussed amongst conductors. The normal practice is to emphasize its three quavers equally, with a tendency for the main emphasis to come automatically on the first. Two bars later, however, as soon as individual instruments begin to play the same phrase in the way in which it is valued in a complete bar, the emphasis naturally comes on the second of the quavers. The contrast between the second version and the first, coming so quickly as it does after the opening bar, is so marked that I find it jars. Moreover, it is difficult to justify intellectually. I have yet to hear the performance, however, in which a conductor tries to reconcile the two.

After André's narrow escape with Beethoven and Brahms, he asked some of the section leaders, as they travelled to the next concert on a special plane, whether they minded him conducting from memory. 'No, Maestro,' one replied, 'so long as you remember it,' adding significantly, 'but if by any chance you don't, let *us* put it right.' That was very wise advice to any conductor from an old hand. What the conductor does when a soloist has a momentary lapse of memory is a more difficult question, which fortunately I have never had to answer in practice. Every conductor prays it may never happen! Perhaps the most effective solution would be to seize one's own score and hold it in front of the soloist with the left hand, while carrying on with the orchestra with the right. This is another reason for never conducting (or, for that matter, accompanying) without a score.

150

Arrangement of an orchestra

The LSO photographed in the Royal Festival Hall and (right) a diagram of its normal layout

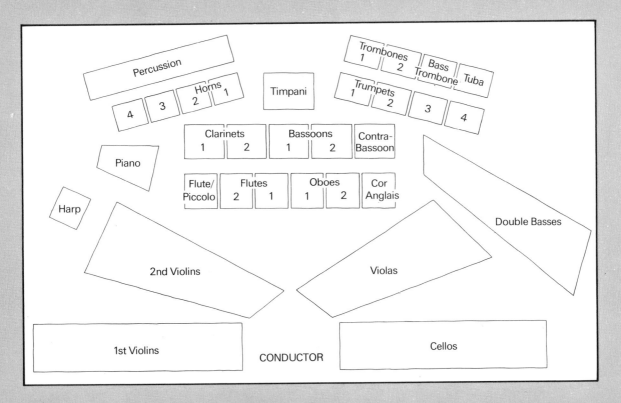

| Percussion | | | | | | Trombones 1 | 2 | Bass Trombone | Tuba |
| 4 | 3 | Horns 2 | 1 | Timpani | | Trumpets 1 | 2 | 3 | 4 |

| Clarinets 1 | 2 | Bassoons 1 | 2 | Contra-Bassoon |

Piano

| Flute/ Piccolo | Flutes 2 | 1 | Oboes 1 | 2 | Cor Anglais |

Harp

Double Basses

2nd Violins

Violas

1st Violins

CONDUCTOR

Cellos

Instruments of the orchestra

The four groups in the orchestral family

Brass
1 Tuba
2 Trumpet
3 Trombone
4 Bass trombone
5 French horn

Percussion
6 Timpani
7 Side drum
8 Bass drum
9 Triangle
10 Cymbals

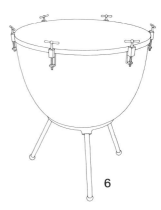

1

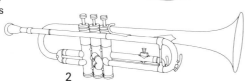

2

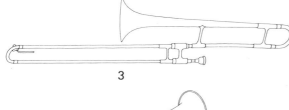

3

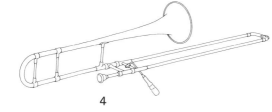

4

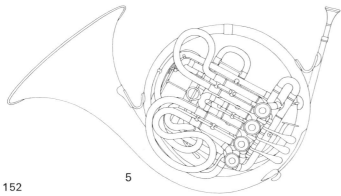

5

6

7

8

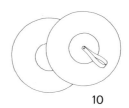

9

10

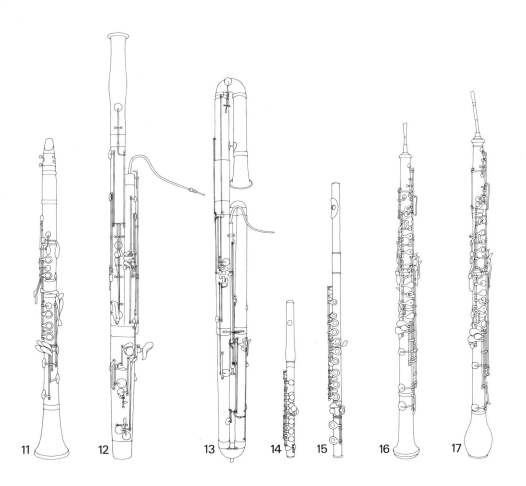

Woodwind
11 Clarinet
12 Bassoon
13 Contrabassoon
14 Piccolo
15 Flute
16 Oboe
17 Cor anglais

Strings
18 Violin
19 Viola
20 Cello
21 Double bass

Conducting movements

Right: The orchestra is ready

The positions for four beats in a bar

1 First beat down
2 Second beat to the left
3 Third beat to the right
4 Fourth beat up

Opposite:

5 Gentle playing from the strings
6 Full orchestral chords
7 The brass – but not too much
8 Precision from the woodwind

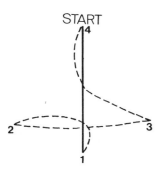

5

6

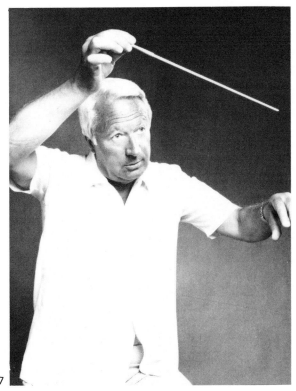

7

8

On tour with the LSO

Right and below: Rehearsing Elgar's 'Cockaigne' Overture in the Gürenich concert hall in Cologne, 10 April 1975

Opposite below: With André Previn, the orchestra's principal conductor, during a break in the rehearsal

I encountered the sort of difficulties which confront an orchestra on tour when we rehearsed in Bonn. André decided that he wanted only a short rehearsal; apart from the rearrangement of the 'Romeo and Juliet' suite the programme was the same as at Cologne the night before, and he thought the orchestra would be fresher if he did not go over all the same ground again. Nevertheless, when we arrived at the Beethoven Halle we found complete confusion. Nothing had been set out for the orchestra on the stage. Some of its members were trying to put their own chairs and stands into position but their efforts were being frustrated by a mass of television technicians trundling their cameras around trying to find the best positions for them among the players, while others were erecting large stands on each side of the stage to carry the cameras looking down on the orchestra. A third platform was being erected in the middle of the hall – which was obviously going to infuriate the audience – and the noise of the hammering and shouting was, to say the least, disconcerting. On top of all this, from time to time a disembodied voice boomed from a large speaker telling the television crews loudly and clearly what was expected of them. It was a scene of complete disorganization, and one of the orchestra members caustically commented: 'At last I know why the Germans didn't win the war.' The hammering having come to an end, André managed to quieten some of the shouting and eventually began the rehearsal; but nothing was able to prevent the raucous voice from still forcefully issuing its instructions. It just had to be ignored.

This particular tour only lasted three days, but after it I was better able to imagine the effects of one lasting three weeks or more; the continuous strain of constant travel, the upsets from eating strange food, the complications of working in a fresh hall each night and the tedium of playing the same programme, or a variant of it, at each concert. Yet these orchestral tours, which have increased so much over the last twenty years, are of immense importance for the listener. The opportunity of hearing great orchestras from other countries enriches our musical lives. My regret is that orchestras – or individual musicians for that matter – so seldom have the opportunity of listening to one another. What could they not learn from such an experience? I would like to be able to take a thousand seats in the Royal Festival Hall so that the ten leading British orchestras could have an evening off – with all fees paid – to listen to the Berlin Philharmonic under Karajan, the Chicago Symphony Orchestra under Solti and the Vienna Philharmonic under Abbado, each showing off the characteristic qualities which have made them so great. Conductors may have more opportunities for concert-going but they seldom seem to take them. Whereas politicians, industrialists and those in the professions follow one another's activities as closely as they can, conductors seem to show little

interest in other conductors' performances; few of them even listen to recordings. Composers are much the same. Perhaps it is because they are so absorbed in their own creative activity, or perhaps they fear that their own conceptions will be unduly influenced by other people's. Whatever the reason, the situation seems unlikely to change.

The relationship between the conductor and the players can vary a great deal with the size of the orchestra and the hall in which they are playing. Perhaps this is more noticeable today than it used to be because of the display which a conductor is so often expected to provide with a full symphony orchestra. When, as a student at Oxford, I heard Felix Weingartner conduct Beethoven's Third Symphony, the 'Eroica', this small balding man had a style so undemonstrative that from the audience one could hardly see his baton moving. Yet his control over the orchestra was complete. His own personal magnetism was immense, but it was reinforced by his very limited physical action: the orchestra knew that any indication given to them would in itself be small in scope but clear and precise. On this occasion they responded to Weingartner's method by producing a really full-blooded performance of the 'Eroica' in which the rhythm was particularly strong. Today the situation is very different: all too often orchestras find themselves having to interpret unbounded physical motion which may be highly rhythmic but is often much more impressionistic in its mode of communication.

When conducting a chamber orchestra – strings, a small number of woodwind and very limited brass, as in Bach's

GALAKONZERT

11. April 1975   20.15 Uhr Gürzenich Köln

12. April 1975   20.15 Uhr Beethovenhalle Bonn

LONDON SYMPHONY ORCHESTRA

Dirigent
ANDRÉ PREVIN

Hector Berlioz   Der Korsar op. 21

Dirigent und Klavier
ANDRÉ PREVIN

Wolfgang Amadeus Mozart   Klavierkonzert Nr. 24 KV 491
Allegro   Larghetto   Allegretto

——— PAUSE ———

Dirigent
EDWARD HEATH

Edward Elgar   Overture Cockaigne op. 40

Dirigent
ANDRÉ PREVIN

Serge Prokofieff   Romeo und Julia
(Musik aus dem Ballet aus den Suiten op. 64 Nr. 1 u. 2)
Introduktion
Die Montagues und die Capulets
Das Mädchen Julia
Maskentanz
Romeos und Julias Grab
Tod des Tybalt

Brandenburg Concertos, for example, or the early Haydn or Mozart symphonies – it is not only possible, but aesthetically desirable, to use what I have described above as the Weingartner technique. In a chamber orchestra the musicians can hear each other playing and much more easily coordinate their phrasing, while the conductor, with a glance or a slight movement of a hand, can bring out whatever he wants in the way of emphasis or light and shade. This was brought home to me when I conducted the English Chamber Orchestra at the concluding concert of the Windsor Festival in October 1975. The entire evening was devoted to Mozart, starting with the lively and amusing overture to *The Escape from the Seraglio* and with the Symphony No. 29 in A Major as the concluding item. This is an enchanting work which I have known for many years and about which I have very clear ideas. It is easy to produce a humdrum performance, for left to itself the music will play itself; but to give it elegance and to bring out the natural feeling which the young Mozart put into it is a more difficult matter which requires detailed rehearsal. We rehearsed from 11 a.m. to 2 p.m. on the Sunday and again from 3 p.m. to 6 p.m., with the concert at 8 p.m.: a strenuous day. At the morning rehearsal, after running through and polishing the *Seraglio* Overture, I concentrated on the Symphony. Over a cup of coffee during the first break, I asked one of the young violin players how he thought it was going. 'Very well,' he replied, 'but I wish you would give up your LSO habits.' 'What do you mean by that?' I asked him, to which he replied, 'Well, I can quite understand that when you are up there with the LSO and three thousand people in the Festival Hall you need to use that long beat and all that energy, but here with us you only need to raise an eyebrow or a finger and we will give you what you want at once.' It was a salutary lesson which I took to heart. On the other hand, there was also something in that rehearsal for the orchestra, and when we had finished more than two hours' hard work, one of the section leaders said to me, 'You know, we must have played Mozart twenty-nine dozens of times, but this is the first occasion for years that we have been made to go through it section by section, and at times bar by bar to get exactly what the conductor wanted.' Normally, without sufficient time for rehearsal, it is difficult for a conductor to secure the reading he has clearly in his heart and mind; he has to make do with the conventional, with as much of his own superimposed upon it as can be managed.

After the Overture, Gina Bachauer played Mozart's Piano Concerto in C Minor. Accompanying a soloist, whether a singer or instrumentalist, on the piano or with an orchestra, is an art in itself. It demands a degree of understanding and a readiness of response from the pianist or conductor which is quite different from the individual personal reading which is their normal approach. Accompanying Gina Bachauer was a remarkable ex-

Felix Weingartner with the Vienna Symphony Orchestra, London 1936

perience. Our overall concept of this concerto was the same; it is a work in a big mould, the shape of which is set by the orchestra in its lengthy opening introduction on the theme which is later taken up by the piano. It is therefore essential that the orchestra's phrasing of the introduction should be the same way as the pianist's later on. The reverse is the case in the quiet, simple slow movement where the piano opens with a delicious tune – which can in itself be phrased in a variety of ways – which the woodwind and the orchestra then emulate. Gina Bachauer's phrasing was so clear that it was a joy to precede or follow her. At the same time, on points of detail she knew exactly what she wanted and we were able to respond accordingly.

After the Concerto and before the Symphony I included the motet 'Exsultate, Jubilate' for soprano solo, which finishes with a glorious burst of praise on the word 'Alleluia' to one of Mozart's finest tunes. I had got to know this when I was organ scholar at Balliol and I had always wanted to accompany it. It is a testing piece, and to achieve Mozart's purpose the 'Alleluia' requires a high soprano voice which can throw off the aria with the greatest freedom, including a joyous top C in the last 'Alleluia'. The young soprano Felicity Lott did just this. Some people said to me when I was planning this programme that a whole evening of Mozart might turn out to be rather monotonous in content. Nothing could have been further from the truth. The contrast between the wit of the *Seraglio* Overture, the emotional depths of the C Minor Piano Concerto, the joyful outpourings of the 'Exsultate, Jubilate', and, finally, the tunefulness and spontaneity of the A Major Symphony, produced a programme which not only showed many different aspects of Mozart's creative personality but was also deeply satisfying. I was delighted when, after the concert, people came up to me to say that they were going away feeling happier than when they had arrived.

More and more is being done in Britain today to enable young people to appreciate music at an early age. For over fifty years the concerts started by Sir Robert Mayer have provided children with an opportunity of hearing short, individual works for orchestra and soloists, preceded by an explanation of what the work is about. I conducted the Fiftieth Anniversary Concert in this series at the Royal Festival Hall at Christmas 1973, a time of year which gave me the chance of including carols in the programme. Accustomed as I am to leading an audience in this sort of concert, it was a fascinating experience to conduct 3,000 children in the Festival Hall and to find out how readily they responded to my request for bold singing, good phrasing and clear diction.

Rossini's overture to his opera *Cenerentola* – 'Cinderella' – was an obvious piece with which to open a Christmas concert for children. It was appropriate that the orchestra was the BBC

At rehearsal with Gina
Bachauer and the English
Chamber Orchestra, Windsor
Festival, 1975

Academy Orchestra, which consists of young musicians training as orchestral players before they embark on a professional career. 'Tom Sawyer's Saturday' by John Dankworth needed no introduction: Mark Twain's words, narrated by Richard Baker, spoke for themselves. As a piece for narrator and orchestra, it is of the same genre as Prokofiev's 'Peter and the Wolf', but in his music Dankworth shows more of the syncopated influence of modern jazz. I also included in the programme one of Handel's organ concerti, No. 4 in A. These concerti are all tuneful works, many of the tunes having been pillaged by Handel from his other compositions. Perhaps the best known is that in B Flat with an opening much akin to the Alleluia Chorus from the *Messiah*. The Fourth Concerto has long been a favourite of mine and I tried to explain to the children the dialogue between the organ and the orchestra in terms of boy meeting girl and what happened thereafter, a simple 'word picture' – many others might equally well have been contrived – which held their attention because it related their own experience as young people to the music.

A word picture of this kind can also often be helpful to those playing instruments in an orchestra, as I found when rehearsing another of the items in this concert, 'The Entrance of the Queen of Sheba' from Handel's *Solomon*, a work for strings, two oboes and bassoons in which the oboes have a prominent and difficult part to play. But to me the strings are not just playing semiquavers one after another, they are simulating the crowd rushing to the vantage points, jostling one another in their eagerness to see the arrival of the Queen, while the oboes are not just oboes playing in thirds together – they are the heralds of the advancing procession. Thought of in this way, this little piece takes on an added attractiveness for younger players.

Moura Lympany playing
César Franck's Symphonic
Variations at the Bournemouth
Symphony Orchestra Gala
Concert, 26 October 1975

My own youthful experiences of music were very much in my mind when I accepted an invitation to conduct the Bournemouth Symphony Orchestra at a gala concert in October 1975 in order to raise funds to establish a new concert hall, rehearsal hall, library and administrative centre. Not only is the orchestra known for its young and enthusiastic membership, but I felt personally indebted to Bournemouth music. As a boy, on holiday near Southampton Water, I had often cycled through the New Forest to Bournemouth to hear Sir Dan Godfrey conduct the Bournemouth Municipal Orchestra at his Wednesday afternoon concerts. I recall particularly one brilliant performance of Rimsky-Korsakov's 'Scheherazade' after which I cycled all the way home for a very late supper.

At the 1975 concert I conducted the first half of the programme, which consisted of Beethoven's Eighth Symphony followed by César Franck's Symphonic Variations for Piano and Orchestra – a lovely work now seldom played – with Moura Lympany as the soloist. Conducting the accompaniment for this work required a quite different approach from that called for by the Mozart piano concerto at Windsor, because of the free-ranging nature of the piece and the opportunities it gives the soloist to change the pace and emphasis. Moura Lympany brought out all its Romantic characteristics and delighted the audience with the scintillating, rippling Finale. The orchestra too enjoyed the concert; one of the youngest members said, as he watched the audience leaving in their dinner jackets and long dresses for the gala champagne supper, 'It's the first time I've seen an audience properly dressed and worthy of the orchestra.' An orchestra cares just as much about its audience as the audience does about the performance.

7 Bravura!

'That memorable night'

39 Tempo, Nobilmente.

39 Tempo, Nobilmente. *(con molto espress.)*

39

+) N.B. The Cornetti must not be prominent.

There can hardly be a musician anywhere in the world who has not wanted to conduct a well-known symphony orchestra, who has not sat in the audience and felt his fingers moving as they itched to wield the baton, or who had not looked up from his chair in the orchestra and thought how much better he could do it than the fellow on the podium. If only the conductor could be just a little indisposed – nothing serious of course, just enough to prevent him going on to the platform – he himself might step into the gap. The orchestra would respond, the audience would be impressed by his assurance, the critics would acclaim him, long-sought recognition would be at hand; his future would be bright. And, after all, it has happened; not very often, but often enough to keep alive every young musician's dream; it was how Toscanini found himself one night taking charge of the performance instead of being on a cellist's desk. No doubt he would have broken through at some time or other but he seized his opportunity and became probably the world's best known conductor.

It had always been my dream, ever since I had begun to conduct a mixed voice choir in my home town of Broadstairs when I was fifteen. As an organ scholar at Oxford I had done my share of conducting with choir and orchestra and once a year since then, at every Christmastide, I had conducted the Town Carol Concert at my home. In recent years this had become nationally known through its coverage on radio and television and had given much pleasure to people far outside our own locality.

How then could I resist when André Previn, the principal conductor of the London Symphony Orchestra, invited me on their behalf to conduct a piece at their Gala Concert? Having at once accepted the invitation, I had to decide on the piece to play.

I chose Elgar's 'Cockaigne' Overture for a number of special reasons. It is a bravura piece which shows off every aspect of the orchestra in its vivid depiction of London as Elgar conceived it. But, by the same token, this Overture, more than any other, can quickly reveal any weakness which may exist in an orchestra, either in the individual players or in the quality of the ensemble – the sympathy and coordination of the various groups of instruments. Elgar himself was always punctilious in specifying every detail he required in the orchestral playing, and to observe these meticulously is demand enough; but the Overture has so many changing themes to represent the ever-changing pattern of London life, and these are so closely woven into one fabric, that without the greatest understanding among the players, and between them and the conductor, the work can fall apart at the seams.

'Cockaigne' was, in fact, the first bravura piece with orchestration of such brilliance to be written in England. It was first performed by the London Symphony Orchestra – another reason for my selecting it. Elgar himself made two recordings of the work, one in 1926 with the Royal Albert Hall Orchestra, the other in 1933, towards the end of his life, with the BBC Orchestra.

Above: Sir Edward Elgar at the time he wrote the 'Cockaigne' Overture, 1900

Opposite: The full score of the culmination of the Overture; the final return of the main theme is marked *'Nobilmente'*

Previous pages: The LSO Gala performance, 25 November 1971 – the sustained *sforzando* chord before the last five bars of 'Cockaigne'

It is extraordinary how widely these two recordings differ. It is well known that composers are very often not the best conductors of their own works because of their difficulty in conveying to the orchestra their real intentions, but for anyone who believes that the composer does nevertheless secure the authentic version of his composition, these two recordings will come as something of a revelation. It is true, though perhaps somewhat surprising, that there are the usual little difficulties in both versions. After coming off the pause in the third bar, for instance, there is a mad scramble by the strings to try to get back to the beat, and again the strings don't quite get the turn after the trill before swinging into the theme for the last time – but what is really so striking is the difference in presentation of the whole work in the two versions.

I chose a 'show-off' piece because it was a gala night. I am one of those who believe that music for a gala really should be something which the audience can both admire and enjoy; it is not an occasion for introducing new works or promoting musical education. Moreover, 'Cockaigne' is about the capital, as its sub-title 'In London Town' states, and this gave it an added appropriateness. There is the bustle of the streets, the warmth of the people, the young lovers strolling through the park and into the church, the military band marching to and from the changing of the guard and later just a hint, in the distance, of the Salvation Army band not altogether in tune; all this goes to make up a sound-picture of the traditional London we know so well.

But there was another reason in my mind at the time, a reason which linked the sort of performance I wanted from the orchestra with the country's state of mind – or, if I may put it this way, with the performance I was trying to elicit from the nation. Let me explain what I mean.

Several years before, in 1963, I had heard the New York Philharmonic Orchestra under Leonard Bernstein play 'Cockaigne' at the Festival Hall as the last item in their programme. Never before had I heard it played so brilliantly and with so much panache. It wasn't only that the orchestra was in tremendous form or that the work suited Bernstein, or Bernstein's style, superbly well; what I felt was that I was hearing it played by people who really believed in themselves and in what they were playing. They had the same attitude as we in Britain had had when the work was written at the beginning of the century, and their 'Cockaigne' contrasted strikingly with the rather lifeless, ironed-out versions to which we had become accustomed. That night I felt that we needed to have the kind of faith in ourselves that this vigorous, buoyant American interpretation seemed to embody. As Prime Minister, I wanted the British to regain their former pride and ebullience, not through empty pomp and circumstance but through the knowledge that deep down they were capable of

Left: Miss Beatrice Harrison at a recording session with Sir Edward Elgar, 15 November 1920

Below: Elgar conducting 'Land of Hope and Glory' at the opening of the Wembley Empire Exhibition, 1924

coping with whatever might come. Perhaps the right performance of 'Cockaigne' could show the way.

I had always loved Elgar's works and in many ways felt an instinctive sympathy with them, though it was not until quite recently that I got a real understanding of the man himself, as a result of reading *Edward Elgar: The Record of a Friendship* by Rosa Barley and Frank C. Carruthers. At Balliol I had played a recording of the First Symphony, following it with a miniature score borrowed earlier from my music master at school and never returned to him. *The Dream of Gerontius* has always seemed to me one of the most glorious and moving works of this century; only with the last pages of Stravinsky's *Symphony of Psalms* have I found myself emotionally stirred in a similar way (and here the music may be striking an echo from the plainsong I sang and accompanied in my youth). *The Kingdom* and *The Apostles* are two of Elgar's mature choral works which have always been underestimated, and infrequently performed, though fortunately there are splendid recordings of both by Sir Adrian Boult and the London Philharmonic Choir and Orchestra. For sheer beauty of sound and purity of vocal line they are difficult to match, and was there ever a more lovely, haunting theme than the Andante after that typical, majestic opening to the introduction of *The Kingdom*? The 'Enigma Variations' combine all that is best in Elgar, his command of melody, his skill in orchestration, his characterization of individual personalities, his ability to weave the threads together into an intricate pattern from which the triumphant conclusion finally emerges.

It is commonly said that Elgar's music is above all English in its nature. That is an over-simplification, no doubt partly deriving from the image which Elgar liked to create of himself as a man of the countryside enjoying sporting life and country ways. But his music is much more than that; it is European in the broadest sense, created before extreme nationalism took hold of the modern nation state. Indeed, much of his work was recognized and acclaimed in Europe before it was widely known in England. The first English performance of *The Dream of Gerontius*, under Hans Richter, in Birmingham was a fiasco but it was then well produced in Germany. It was there too that the 'Enigma Variations' and the First Symphony were given repeated performances before they were firmly established at home. Today, Elgar's music is accepted internationally and will become more and more so, but it was the European aspect of his work which appealed to me that night at the Gala Concert – just after we had successfully negotiated Britain's entry into the EEC.

But to return to the concert. I had my first rehearsal with the orchestra the day before the performance. The sheet sent out from the LSO office showed that the orchestra was rehearsing the rest of the programme from 2.30 p.m. onwards; I was summoned for 4.30 p.m. and allocated the last hour of the afternoon.

Fortunately, the rehearsal was in the Festival Hall itself; fortunately, because it would enable me to judge the balance of the orchestra in the hall in which the concert would take place. This is unusual for the penultimate rehearsal of a London orchestra. Indeed, it is the curse permanently upon most of our London orchestras that they have to rehearse in a number of halls widely dispersed over the capital, none of them bearing any relationship acoustically to the hall in which the performance is to take place. In the case of the London Symphony Orchestra and the London Philharmonic Orchestra this has now happily been changed by the conversion of a disused church, Holy Trinity Church, Southwark, into a permanent rehearsal centre. I was delighted to find that I would not have to face the horrors of rehearsing in some unsuitable, outlandish hall.

When I arrived at the rehearsal, I found the orchestra having their break after the first part of the programme and ready to begin on 'Cockaigne'. After clapping for silence, André Previn said a few words of introduction, after which I took over. Handling a rehearsal is far from easy. Nothing is more important for the conductor than to know precisely what he wants in the performance of a work and exactly how he proposes to get it. Ideally, the rehearsal should lead to a work being so well prepared that at the performance the orchestra plays its way through the work without the conductor having to keep adjusting everything as he goes along. What a fallacy it is to think that the man up there on the podium always busily ssshing here and shouting there is really doing an effective job as conductor: that ought to have been done long before. All too often on the night it is a mark

With André Previn after rehearsing the 'Cockaigne' Overture. Robert Armstrong, my private secretary, is holding the score and my baton

of under-rehearsal or over-fussiness – or both. But to reach the
ideal state I have described – and the few really great performances I have heard in my life have been like that – it is essential
to be able to organize the rehearsal properly and to make the
fullest use of the always limited time available. The conductor
must know clearly in his mind what he wants to obtain from it
and how he intends to apportion the time he has been allotted.
The orchestra will take endless pains over some particular part
of the piece, in order to get exactly what the conductor requires,
provided they can understand what he is driving at. Nothing
both infuriates and bores them more than when he appears to be
going again and again over the same extract to no particular
purpose.

I have always believed in explaining my conception of a work
to the choir or orchestra at the beginning of a rehearsal, and
I did so on this occasion. I suspect that the orchestra was gently
taken aback at what may at first have appeared to be presump-
tuous and unsolicited advice to the group on whom Elgar himself
had relied. But I had a purpose. I wanted to conjure up in their
minds the imagery Elgar was trying to convey. I wanted to get
that extra bit of bounce into the Londoner in the opening bars.
I wanted that extra richness in the luscious, flowing tune conveying the confident splendour of Edwardian London. I wanted that
extra touch of gentleness for the lovers as they strolled through

the park and into the church. I wanted the horns to think of themselves as an organ when they played the soft reflective music there; an organ with the swell pedal gently opening and closing but without changing the smooth passage of the music. And just before the band arrived, I wanted no ordinary up and down scales on the strings but the real bustle and excitement of a crowd as they jostled on the pavement craning their necks and pushing their neighbours forward in their attempts to see the guardsmen as they came into view; above all, I wanted the great swelling tune to lead to a climax such as there had never been before.

The orchestra listened patiently and we set off on the overture. I told them we would do a straight run-through first – just to see how it went – and then we would come back to work through it bit by bit. I say 'we set off', but first we had to get that start right on the fourth beat of the first bar. It may give some satisfaction to say 'at least we all finished together' but there is nothing more vital than the start – and in some works nothing more tricky. It is essential for the beat to give the right speed from the very first note. There is nothing worse than setting off at too slow or too fast a pace and having to adjust as soon as you are under way. In any case, 'Cockaigne' has only one and a quarter bars before the orchestra is thrown into a pause at the beginning of the third bar, after which you have to get back to your original speed again. There are two ways of doing this. One is to bring the strings

straight in on the actual beat of their entry: this I always like to do, but it does mean that the whole orchestra only has a glimpse of a slight movement of the baton from which to get the speed you want before they are in on the beat and away. In this case, however, the leader of the orchestra suggested the alternative solution. 'They would prefer you,' he said, 'actually to beat out the whole of the bar in which they come in so that they can be absolutely sure of the tempo.'

Everyone sees the leader of the orchestra come on before the conductor, take his applause and occupy his seat as the first violin. What does he really do? What functions does he perform before that moment when the spotlight falls upon him? (Incidentally, in most orchestras outside Britain, the leader actually leads the orchestra on to the platform and takes no individual applause, stands for the tuning of the orchestra until he is satisfied all is well and then takes his seat with the rest of the orchestra in silence while they await the conductor. I rather think that is a better way of doing it.) Of course, in those orchestral works where there is a violin solo, for example in the Benedictus in Beethoven's Mass in D or in Richard Strauss's tone poem '*Heldenleben*', the leader will play it, and such solos provide a wonderful opportunity to display his own talent; but behind the scenes during rehearsals he has other important tasks. Each section of the orchestra has its own leader, and very often deputy leader, responsible for ensuring co-ordination within the group. The leader of the orchestra does this for the first violins and overall for the rest of the strings as well. He also provides an essential link between the conductor and the whole of the orchestra on any particular problems of technique which may arise.

When the leader of the orchestra said that the players would prefer me to beat out the whole bar, I naturally took his advice – and then we got under way. That was a good rehearsal, nearly an hour packed full of hard work. My introductory words had paid off, and one of the orchestra was heard commenting as he went away at the end: 'I have played this thing dozens of times but I learned more from him of what it is really about than I learned from all the previous rehearsals and performances put together.' I had to work hard at individual passages that evening because I knew that the time allocated to me for the rehearsal the following morning, the day of the concert, was very short. Above all, I had to pay constant attention to the balance of the orchestra. This always brings immense difficulties because the conductor is at the centre of the sound, whether it be the softest murmur he can cajole or the wildest furore he can control, and yet he has to achieve a balance which will be maintained throughout the concert hall. Nowhere is this more testing than in the Festival Hall in London. It is always described as 'dry' – in other words, lacking in resonance. A real degree of resonance gives richness to orchestral sound; it can at the same time hide many a mistake.

Programme

**ELGAR
OVERTURE: COCKAIGNE**
Conducted by Edward Heath

**PREVIN
GUITAR CONCERTO**
World Première
Soloist, John Williams

INTERVAL

**SIBELIUS
VIOLIN CONCERTO IN
D MINOR, Op. 47**
Soloist, Isaac Stern

**BERNSTEIN
OVERTURE: CANDIDE**

No orchestra can afford to take the Festival Hall for granted, least of all one used to playing under resonant conditions, for here every single line of music is clearly audible and balance becomes all the more important. The utmost precision and the most careful balance between instruments are required.

The London Symphony Orchestra, of course, is used to playing at the Festival Hall; moreover, as an orchestra it is young, interested, intelligent and quick to respond to the demands made upon it. My main problem that evening was to convey to them what I wanted. I knew what I wanted – the problem was how to get it. Was I overawed by such a task? Looking back on it, yes. Perhaps that made me rather stiff and wooden; my conducting at that first rehearsal was quite unlike the relaxed, adaptable style I had always cultivated. Nevertheless, I went home well content, feeling that we had made good progress.

The rehearsal the next morning was at 10 o'clock. I had only been allocated a quarter of an hour, a few minutes longer than the length of the overture itself. The previous evening I had gone through the score again and made a note of the points where I still felt I had not got it quite right. I started by telling the orchestra about these specific problems and then proceeded to rehearse each in turn. It was only then that I had a final rehearsal of the complete work. This, of course, was reversing the order of the previous evening. The complete run-through went extremely well, so well in fact that I wondered if it could go as well on the night. André Previn then took over to rehearse the rest of the concert and I went back to No. 10 to get on with my day's work.

First there was a meeting of the Cabinet, over which I presided. Starting at 11 o'clock, it lasted until 1.15 p.m. Then, after a quick lunch, I had a meeting with my private secretaries about the questions I had to answer in the House of Commons that afternoon. At 3 o'clock I went across to the House and dealt with questions, both those of which notice had been given and all the supplementaries which followed. I then had to sit and listen through the first part of the debate on Northern Ireland after which I went back to No. 10 for some other meetings. It was 7 o'clock before I could go up to my flat to change into a white tie ready to go to the Festival Hall. 'Quite a day's programme, one way and another,' I thought to myself as I was getting ready. 'Quite a contrast with other conductors, who could go off for a rest and a sleep between their final rehearsal and the concert!' No matter, there had been no time to worry about further details in the score, or whether everything would go as planned. It had been an extraordinary day, in fact, but then not often does a prime minister in office carry out such an extraordinary assignment as to conduct one of the world's great symphony orchestras in a gala concert.

In the Festival Hall they had allocated me a 'green room' to myself. There for some time I sat in solitary state. Everyone obviously thought that before a concert the occupant should be left alone. However, things gradually began to happen. The orchestra librarian came to collect my score to put on the stand. I asked him to see that it was at the height I had measured that morning, and with the right tilt. Isaac Stern, an old friend, who was playing the Sibelius Violin Concerto in the concert, put his head round the door to enquire how I was. While we were chatting, André Previn appeared to tell me that he was going on first to introduce me; afterwards the concert manager appeared to say he would give me the cue when to leave my room and when actually to go on the stage.

By this time it was almost 8 o'clock and everyone suddenly disappeared. A few more minutes alone in reflection and then came the light tap on the door and the concert manager's voice: 'We will now go to the edge of the platform so that you can hear what André says.' Together we sat by the curtain which hid us from the packed hall. 'A lot of money in the house tonight, Sir,' said one of the attendants. The curtain was drawn aside and André Previn went up the steps to the platform to the loud applause which always greets him. His few witty remarks did something to relax an audience which was tense with anticipation – or should I say curiosity? – but was not at all certain what it was about to see happen. Then I got my cue and went on to join André, happy that all the preliminaries were almost at an end. At this point I really wished we were going to open with the National Anthem, just to relieve some of the nervous tension I felt and which I was sure the orchestra shared. It certainly had that effect when, some years later, I conducted a gala performance of the Bournemouth Symphony Orchestra; but tonight we had to go straight into 'Cockaigne'.

I gave the orchestra their three preliminary beats and off we went, just at the speed I wanted. Came the pause and then we were safely out of that and away again. We broadened out into the first splendid theme and suddenly I realized how fully the orchestra, together and as individuals, were responding to me. I felt I could do almost anything I wanted with them. Behind me the concentration of the audience was intense. They, too, would follow wherever we led. And so to the delicacy of the young lovers; and when it came to that arpeggio of the cellos, as we reached the end of the scene, I could not help but dally over each note. The cellos were relishing every moment, how the brass enjoyed themselves later, what precision, what fullness of sound, yet still not overwhelming the rest of the orchestra. Then came the development of all the themes together, the orchestra gradually piling crescendo upon crescendo before suddenly dissolving into the woodwind's merry Cheeky Chappie cockney tune. I found myself laughing with delight at this vibrant chorus. And so we swept into that last glorious burst of Elgar's major theme, symbolizing all that went to make up the overwhelming sense of prosperity and stability in Edwardian London. A bit of a tricky turn into it, the brass broadening out, horns, trumpets and trombones marching down, the top strings and flutes madly trilling away double forte, and now, in the second half of the last bar before the theme, the trumpets and horns heavily emphasizing every half beat as the music dramatically slowed until with a quick little turn – and a flip of the page – the whole orchestra took up the tune. '*Nobilmente*', Elgar marked it, and '*nobilmente*' it was going to be. The organ crashed in for the first time, the top strings – *con molto espressione* – were putting all they had got into it, as instrument after instrument took it up until finally, in ever descending scales, we came to those two great resonant chords – how accurate they were tonight, split-second timing, a smashing emphasis on the beginning of each – and so into the last five bars. Then back to the very first theme of the overture, but

no longer softly on the first violins – this time the whole orchestra whipping it out. They remembered what we had done to it at rehearsal. All too often these two bars sound like an anti-climax in performance, a let-down after that grand theme, but tonight they were being thrown out by the orchestra with brilliant abandon, like a fistful of rockets breaking out together in the sky. The man on the timpani comes into his own; fourteen quavers of ever-increasing intensity, punctuated by two chords from the orchestra, the second becoming louder and louder until the timpanist led us with four blood-tingling beats into the final crashing chord of the overture. The applause burst out. It was Gala Concert night for the London Symphony Orchestra in the Royal Festival Hall on 25 November 1971, and what a thrill it had been. As Prime Minister of Great Britain I had conducted one of the world's greatest symphony orchestras. How much so many others would have given to have had that opportunity. How fortunate I was.

Afterwards the critics were all agog to find out from members of the orchestra what it had been really like. 'Gives us time to breathe,' said one wind player, 'not like those whizz kids who rush through everything from one end to the other. I suppose it's because he's used to conducting choirs a lot. They need time to breathe as well.' 'It takes an Englishman to conduct Elgar, you know,' said one of the strings, 'they all try him nowadays but only an Englishman really understands Elgar.' The critics didn't get much to latch on to and the following morning they were extremely kind.

The concert was recorded, and EMI issued the record shortly afterwards. It has sold all over the world and will still be in the catalogue in 1977 – six years is not bad for a classical recording of that kind. The first time I played it I suddenly realized how different it sounds in the concert hall and in one's own sitting room. I had been able to do things in the Festival Hall, in the atmosphere of that Gala Concert with a responsive orchestra and a highly strung audience, which one would never even have thought of doing when recording in a studio. It only goes to show that there is a difference between the real thing and a recording, even a live one. There was another surprise in store for me, however: when I turned over the record for the rest of the programme, I found that the concert performance had disappeared. When I enquired what had happened, I found that André Previn had taken the LSO off to the EMI studio the following week and had recorded the other works there. They had not had to rely on one performance straight through, deal with the acoustics of the hall or put up with the odd cough in the background. 'André,' I said when I next saw him, 'you've cheated!' And so he had, but I am always glad that my recording is the one taken on that memorable night, with all its flaws. It is a recording of what for me will always remain an exciting occasion.

With André Previn and the orchestra at the Gala Concert

8 Record collecting

'The satisfaction to be gained from playing records is almost limitless'

For me, collecting records is a delight in itself, and playing them has many advantages over concert-going. I choose what I want to hear, when I want to hear it; I can make my own programme to suit my mood and to fit my time-table; if I wish, I can stop the recording and replace it with another by a different artist, just to see how they compare; and, last but not least, I can concentrate purely on the music and its performance without any of the distractions of the concert hall. Even in the case of opera and ballet, the absence of the visual element enables me to appreciate the musical content to a greater degree than would otherwise be possible, and for this reason I have often found it helpful to listen to a recording of an opera before I see it for the first time; conversely, when I know an opera well I can visualize the scene as I listen to a recording. Moreover, the incredibly high level of expertise which has now been developed, not only in the recording process but in the technique of cutting and bonding together tapes, takes us nearer to perfection than is usually the case in live performance. When I went to listen to the preparatory disc of the Robert Mayer Concert for Children which I conducted at the Festival Hall in December 1973, I was shown at the same time the process of editing together extracts from successive recordings of an operatic tenor aria. So finely cut was this tape and so determined was the producer on perfection that the introductory note to the aria was taken from one version and used to replace a slightly off-timbre note in what was otherwise by far the best recording. Hearing it played through, I could not detect a break or alteration of any kind.

Of course, none of this is to say that a recording can ever completely replace a live performance. The atmosphere in the concert hall or opera house, the personalities of those taking part, the interaction between the audience and the performers, all give live performances a character of their own which cannot be reproduced in the studio. Nor can they be retained in recordings of live performances; indeed, all that the latter tends to do is to reveal more clearly the kind of imperfection one often fails to notice in the concert hall, where one's attention is held by the general momentum of the music. In the last analysis it will always be the live performance which really matters; nevertheless, the satisfaction to be gained from playing records is almost limitless.

Equipment
Buying equipment on which to play records is a matter requiring specialist advice, something which I would not presume to give in detail. Only the expert can advise on the merits and demerits of stereo and quadraphonic systems, cassettes and tapes. All I can do is to pass on the benefits of my own experience. My first stereo set was given to me by my constituency supporters to celebrate my tenth year as a Member of Parliament. The complete unit, including speakers, was designed and made by one manufacturer.

What was important was that those buying the equipment had carefully measured the size of the room in which it was to be played. This is vital as a first step in deciding upon your equipment. It then becomes a question of which appeals to you most in reproductive quality and is within the price range you can afford. There is no point in buying a machine with a power far greater than that required for your sitting room, for it will have to be kept toned down all the time, it will sound remote, and the immediacy and the liveliness of the reproduction will suffer. On the other hand, you will feel frustrated by the inadequacy of a machine which cannot fill the room with sound around you while you listen. After I had had my first stereo for five years, I changed it for one more suitable for the high ceiling of the room in my flat in Albany. This time the experts put together a set composed of the individual units which they judged best for each purpose, a pick-up by one manufacturer, a turntable by another and an amplifier and speakers by a third. Selecting this equipment and setting it up in the room obviously required special technical knowledge, and I was content to leave this side of the operation to the experts. My task was to form a judgement on the quality and balance of the reproduction once the system was installed. In order to do this I tried out several different kinds of recording. The piano is always my first test, to find out whether there is a faithful reproduction of its sound, always the most difficult to achieve. Next I try a high soprano voice, because this is most likely to reveal any distortion in the upper register of the loudspeakers. After that, I put on a piece of symphonic music to judge the instrument's capacity for reproducing full orchestral sound. Finally, I put on an organ record, because even though the equipment may have passed all the other tests the full sound of the organ with its thirty-two-foot pipes will reveal any low distortion or loss of depth. My present equipment passed all these tests successfully and it has served me well now for more than ten years. Having taken time off a couple of years ago to try out new loudspeakers that had come on to the market in the meantime, including some that I could not possibly have afforded, I remain satisfied that I cannot improve on what I have got.

Starting a collection

How, then, should you start a record collection? The answer is, go for what you like. Don't worry about getting the things you think you ought to have; buy a record of something you have heard and enjoyed, made perhaps by the people you first heard playing it. Later you will want to listen to versions by different artists before finally making your choice. Of course this takes time, especially where concertos, symphonic music or opera are concerned; moreover, it is difficult to carry the difference in performance in one's head when listening to a series of recordings, especially if there has to be a week's interval between each one.

The alternative is to rely on other people's descriptions of the recordings, however contradictory they may be at times. I always follow record reviews in the press and in the monthly issues of the *Gramophone*. In addition, there is the monthly letter from EMG which gives detailed evaluations and each year I get *The Art of Record Buying*, which summarizes the existing repertoire. A third way of handling the problem is to try to pick out from the reviews the recording likely to appeal to you most and then to hear that through in the shop before you finally buy it. With experience you will come to know which artists produce the sort of performance you like for individual instruments, particular composers or certain kinds of works. No one else can satisfactorily make those decisions for you – and after all a great deal of the fun of record collecting is reading about new records, listening to some of them, and making up one's mind.

Your first records

If you want suggestions, why not start with a record of some ballet music? Its tuneful, bewitching, orchestral sound is the sort of thing that stays with you after you have heard it and makes you feel more light-hearted. One of the first records I bought was the music for 'Les Sylphides', a collection of Chopin pieces beautifully orchestrated in a suite. Two works originally written for ballet, Tchaikovsky's 'Sleeping Beauty' and 'Nutcracker', were also among my early favourites. Both have memorable tunes and luscious orchestration. Later on, I hope you will also be attracted by contemporary ballet music such as Prokofiev's 'Lieutenant Kijé' and 'Romeo and Juliet', both of which have been arranged in suites by the composer.

After ballet music I would suggest that you try some vocal records. I began by buying a record of Joan Sutherland, that magnificent Australian soprano, singing various operatic arias. I found these so good that I then bought the second record in the series, 'The Art of the Prima Donna'. Since then, I have added a number of a similar kind – one of Maria Callas which I particularly like contains arias from Verdi operas; another of Montserrat Caballé Puccini arias, and one of Beverly Sills (who sang at the reception for me at the White House) singing Bellini and Donizetti arias. Leontyne Price singing five great operatic scenes on one record led me to her other one with Mozart arias on it. I have Victoria de los Angeles singing songs from many countries, but particularly Spain, and Janet Baker giving a French recital. Tito Gobbi, who came down to Chequers, has put together on one record arias recorded since 1942, first rate in themselves and of great historical interest. My most recent addition of this kind is a record of Elly Ameling, which not only contains Mozart's 'Exsultate, jubilate' but also an excellent selection of arias and songs by Bach, Handel, Mozart, Schubert and Hugo Wolf. On a lighter note, 'Love live forever' contains two recordings of Joan Sutherland singing, with orchestra and chorus, gems from musical comedy. What a difference it makes to have these well sung.

Similarly, in piano music, there are many records containing a variety of compositions played by the same artist. One of Artur Rubinstein's contains the Brahms piano pieces which appeal to him most; Vladimir Horowitz has done the same for Chopin. Svjatoslav Richter has recorded a programme ranging from early Haydn to late Prokofiev; and 'Richter in Italy' is a live recording of a concert of Schumann. Moura Lympany, one of our finest women pianists, has recorded famous classics for the piano, which gives a very good idea of the variety of piano pieces available.

I think you will find it is useful to buy records of this kind to begin with so that it is possible to decide on what to concentrate later. But when a record contains a selection of pieces there is no reason why one should play it all through at one go. This is particularly true in the case of vocal arias, and it applies even more to selections of orchestral overtures. There are a number of excellent records entirely devoted to overtures – Bernstein's Beethoven Overtures or von Karajan's Beethoven Overtures in his 'Music for the Theatre', Toscanini's Rossini Overtures and Bruno Walter's Mozart Overtures, for example – but however good each one may be there is not much satisfaction to be gained from playing a whole series of them one after the other. In any case, overtures do not provide the best introduction to orchestral music; instead I would suggest that you try some of the Dance Suites and Serenades of Bach, Handel and Mozart for strings or small orchestra. These were all composed for special functions at court or elsewhere and they have a characteristic liveliness which is very stimulating. They are tuneful, not too long, and can be fitted into any programme. Yehudi Menuhin's recordings of many of these with the Bath Festival Orchestra I find very happy ones. Handel's 'Water Music' and 'Music for the Royal Fireworks', now available in an excellent recording by Neville Marriner and the Academy of St Martin-in-the-Fields, are more extended works, but full of gaiety and lively tunes. Mozart's '*Eine kleine Nachtmusik*' is more sophisticated; I still love my old recording by Bruno Walter, but there are many others to choose from.

Chamber Music

Perhaps you should now make a start on trios and quartets – ideal music for those quiet moments at the end of the day when you feel the need for repose. I began my collection with a charming quartet by Haydn, No. 57 in G Major Opus 54 No. 1 played by the Amadeus Quartet, and another by Mozart, No. 20 in D Major, K.499, 'The Hoffmeister', performed by the Vienna Philharmonic Quartet. I doubt whether anyone could fail to enjoy these. Both composers wrote an ample number of quartets from which to choose. I have already given vent to my enthusiasm for Beethoven's 'Archduke' Trio Opus 97 and Schubert's B Flat Trio. I can only give my own preference for these recordings, as in all the others I mention. For both the 'Archduke' and the Schubert B Flat Trio I have constantly played the recordings by the David Oistrakh Trio and the more recent ones by Isaac Stern and his trio. In the Schubert the Oistrakh Trio make what I would describe as a 'natural' approach. Isaac Stern's trio is much more pointed and some may feel that they get more out of it. The classic performance of the Schubert Trio is that by Cortot, Thibaud and Casals recorded in 1926 which I now have in its re-recorded form for stereo. Those who have enjoyed any of these performances will also want to buy a recording of Schubert's Piano Quintet in A Major, 'The Trout', which has the same effervescent characteristics as the Trio. My version is by Clifford Curzon with members of the Vienna Octet. In the fourth movement the piano represents the bubbling brook, repeating the accompaniment to Schubert's song of the same name as the Quintet, 'Die Forelle'. Individual songs by Schubert make an excellent starting point for those who want to collect *Lieder*. Many of these – Schubert's 'Erlkönig' or 'Heidenröslein', for example – will already be familiar; others such as Schumann's 'Die Rose, die Lilie' from the 'Dichterliebe' are just as enchanting. My recording of these love songs to Heinrich Heine's words is by Peter Pears and Benjamin Britten.

Chamber music, of course, offers many opportunities for further exploration, and although you may not want to pursue these until later, for the sake of convenience I shall mention some of them here. There are, for instance, Beethoven's middle and late quartets, beginning with the first 'Razumovsky', or his sonatas for violin and piano. Here the 'Spring' Sonata in F and the 'Kreutzer' Sonata, so often on the same disc, provide a good combination. It is easy to pick out the big Beethoven piano sonatas, the 'Moonlight', the 'Waldstein' and the 'Appassionata', but we should not forget such a major work as the Sonata in F Sharp, Opus 78; and many of the others have beautiful individual movements. I prefer Michelangeli's performance of Beethoven's last sonata, Opus 111, above all others; its clarity, poise and restraint give it a spiritual quality worthy of Beethoven's concluding notes.

After Beethoven come Schubert's sonatas; these have all been recorded by Paul Badura-Skoda, while Gilels and Wilhelm Kempff have also made excellent recordings of the A Minor Sonata and the 'Posthumous' Sonata in B Flat respectively. And after these might come the major piano works of Liszt and Brahms; Liszt in many ways impressionistic, and Brahms, in his two sets of Variations on a Theme of Handel and a Theme of Paganini, requiring a virtuosity which only the greatest can produce. Still thinking of music written to be played in our homes there are delightful recordings of little-heard works such as Boccherini's Quintet in C major – part of the first movement reappears at the end of the last movement – and Hummel's Quintet in C Major: music not of the same quality, but entertaining. Mozart's Clarinet Quintet – his Concerto for Clarinet and Orchestra is also very agreeable – and Brahms's Clarinet Quintet, both played by members of the Vienna Octet, are in my record collection. These lead us on quite naturally to Mozart's Quintet in G Minor, Schubert's Quintet in C Major, Mendelssohn's Octet and Brahms's Sextet. All works of quality, I have them recorded by Heifetz, Piatigorsky and their friends at their own concerts. They really are superb.

Concertos

After chamber music it is natural to think of the concertos. Of those for the violin, perhaps Mendelssohn's is the most immediately appealing, although several of Mozart's concertos for the violin are easy on the ear. Beethoven, Brahms and Tchaikovsky all wrote concertos in the virtuoso tradition. Elgar, Sibelius and Walton were more concerned with the soloist being at one with the orchestra than in showing off their technique against it. For the cello we have Haydn's cheerful Concerto in C and one which is usually attributed to him in D, both pleasant works. Dvořák's Cello Concerto has a character and dimension all of its own, especially when forcefully played by Rostropovich. Elgar's Cello Concerto, on the other hand, beautifully played by Jacqueline du Pré, has a reticence which is quite different. There are few works for the viola in concerto form, but William Walton's, played by Yehudi Menuhin, has a quality about it that makes it one of his most deeply penetrating works.

Piano concertos can be said to begin with the harpsichord pieces of Bach, now often transferred to the piano; then come the attractive and straightforward concertos of Haydn and the wonderfully moulded masterpieces of Mozart, whose last piano concertos have an emotional depth the expression of which needs an understanding far transcending the technical requirements set by the composer. Then there are Beethoven's five concertos, the first two always delightful to hear, the Third marking a great step forward in compositions of this kind. The Fourth has long been one of my favourites, but always one comes eventually to the Fifth, truly an 'Emperor' among concertos. Here, the most difficult moment of all is in the transition from the end of the slow movement to the beginning of the last fiery Rondo. There are few pianists, however great, who pass that test. Claudio Arrau is one of them, and I would recommend his recording. Then there are the very well-known concertos by Schumann and Grieg, Rachmaninov's three concertos and his Variations on a Theme of Paganini: any of these could make a suitable starting-point for a collection, and I would also recommend the lesser-known First Piano Concerto of Mendelssohn, which has an irrepressible gaiety about it. Alternatively, there is the Fourth Piano Concerto of Saint-Saëns with a great thumping tune in its last movement. I have it in a recording by Casadesus which invariably puts me into a buoyant mood. There are then the two concertos of Liszt, both bravura works. César Franck's Symphonic Variations also make a good beginning for a collection. The two piano concertos of Brahms are giants; it has taken me many years since I first heard them in my Oxford days to appreciate fully the wealth of music stored in them. I play Clifford Curzon's recording of the First and Richter's of the Second. In our own century, Prokofiev's Fourth Concerto has made its mark, together with that of Ravel. Few others have become established. The age of the virtuoso pianist-composer appears to be over and the piano is resuming its place once again amongst the rest of the orchestral family.

Symphonies

Here the choice is just as varied. Perhaps Mozart's early Symphony No. 29 in A Major is a suitable starting-point, while Haydn's later symphonies such as the 'Surprise' or the 'Clock' are admirable examples of the symphonic form in its early stages. For sheer pleasure, Mendelssohn's 'Italian' Symphony is, I think, hard to beat, and I also like very much César Franck's Symphony. Although many would describe it as 'wallowing in emotion', this did not stop Sir Thomas Beecham from frequently including it in his programmes. Another very different favourite of Beecham's was Bizet's early 'Little' Symphony in C, which is reminiscent of Schubert's happy music in his Third and Fifth Symphonies. Schubert's 'Unfinished' Symphony has probably been almost worked to death but I still think the second movement to be one of the loveliest he ever wrote.

These, of course, are all comparatively minor works. The great symphonies, on the other hand, hardly need recommending, so general is their acceptance. We know that they contain much of what is finest in Western music, and it is up to us gradually to collect them and assimilate them as we feel we can. As far as I am concerned Mozart, Beethoven, Schubert, Brahms, Tchaikovsky, Dvořák, Bruckner, Mahler and Elgar can meet my needs; after these, it is to Walton, Prokofiev and Shostakovich I turn.

Opera

Collecting the larger works often involves considerable expenditure, and here more than anywhere else it is best to make sure that one will enjoy what one buys. Opera has the great advantage that very often recording companies produce a single disc with a selection of highlights from a complete recording. I never hesitate to buy these in the first instance if they are available. My record of highlights from what is probably the most famous recording of *Der Rosenkavalier* with Elisabeth Schwarzkopf, Christa Ludwig and Teresa Stich Randall taking the main parts with Von Karajan conducting was almost worn thin before I could afford the complete opera. Now there is Georg Solti's splendid version to stand next to it.

187

One problem, not only with opera but with choral works, symphonies and concertos, is that often the complete series of a composer's works is played or conducted by a single artist. Karl Böhm, for example, has produced recordings of a very high quality of all Mozart's major operas; von Karajan has recorded all Beethoven's and Brahms's symphonies; Wilhelm Kempff all Beethoven's piano concertos; Szell and the Cleveland Symphony Orchestra Mozart's last six symphonies; Solti with the London Symphony, Chicago Symphony and the Amsterdam Concertgebouw Orchestras Mahler's nine symphonies – and so on. Should one buy these collected works, or should one pick and choose? It is a difficult problem to settle, though sometimes it settles itself when one can only buy them in the box. To have the works produced by a single artist does very often give them a unity which they would not otherwise have; but often a different artist comes nearest to one's own interpretation of each individual work.

Personally I enjoy Klemperer's version of *The Magic Flute* and Giulini's *Don Giovanni*. Beecham's *Seraglio* is still hard to beat, Solti's comparatively new *Così fan tutte* I find excellent, and Böhm's *Figaro* is a classical Mozart performance. Abbado's recording of Rossini's *Cenerentola* has a precision and diamond-like glitter which is unique. The recordings of the operas of Bellini and Donizetti are a means of showing off the voices of such great sopranos as Joan Sutherland, Montserrat Caballé and Beverly Sills.

The recordings of Verdi's early and middle period operas can be judged very largely on those singing them, whereas for *Otello* and *Falstaff* my preference is very clearly for von Karajan's for the former and Solti's for the latter.

In recent years concentration on Wagner's *Ring* has been intense. Again, Sir Georg Solti's complete recording is a magnificent series. For *Tristan and Isolde* I play Böhm's, though I also have von Karajan's whose *Die Meistersinger*, the result of his production at Salzburg, is simply splendid. Karajan has also recorded Beethoven's *Fidelio* after a Salzburg production and, by any standards, this is a first-rate performance. But I still find myself going back to my Klemperer recording, the first complete one of an opera I ever bought. Perhaps it is because I have played it so often and know it so well that I like to return to it, but listening to it as impartially as I can, I still think it has a dignity combined with passion which make it outstanding.

Choral Works

The great choral works present something of a problem in that very few of them can be reduced to highlights on a disc. Yet how rewarding they are if we are able to give them the time they deserve. Bach's Mass in B Minor is one of the great works of all time. Its structure, its intensity, its emotion, its faith, all require the work to be heard as a whole if it is to make its full effect. His *St Matthew Passion* and the *St John Passion* are of a similar kind.

Handel's *Messiah* is now being recorded in its original form rather than in the version for massed choirs so popular in the last century; of his other works, I find *Israel in Egypt*, of which there are now several good recordings, the one most worth listening to. Beethoven's *Missa Solemnis* in Klemperer's recording was one of the first choral works I bought, as were Mendelssohn's *Elijah*, a favourite with choral societies, and Brahms's *German Requiem*. Elgar's *Dream of Gerontius* I would regard as essential, while his two other major choral works, *The Kingdom* and *The Apostles*, both authoritatively recorded by Sir Adrian Boult, certainly merit attention. Finally I would also recommend one delightful small work, Rossini's *Stabat Mater*, which is almost operatic in its style. I heard this for the first time in Seville at Easter 1964; I wish it were performed more often in this country.

Further aspects of collecting

We are lucky today that some record companies are now putting out in long-playing form important recordings of earlier years. Most of these are of mainly historical interest, but many feature performances which are extremely worth while in themselves. I am thinking particularly of the reissues of the recordings of Toscanini and Horowitz. To those of us who heard little of them in their prime, these are a revelation. Horowitz's recordings of Beethoven's 'Emperor' Concerto and, with Toscanini, Brahms's Second Piano Concerto in B Flat, are magnificent performances, unique in their breadth and conception and technical brilliance.

Even where such recordings have not been reissued it is surprising how many of the originals still survive. I myself have kept all the 78s I accumulated while I was at Oxford; after the war, when I was stationed in Hanover, I was able to buy records from the Polydor Company; and more recently I have begun to go out of my way to acquire recordings of this kind. In this I have been aided by my friends who, not wishing to give me something I have already got, have searched around for the unusual.

There is also a place in my collection for recordings which celebrate great occasions, either of personal interest – musical or otherwise – or important because of their association with artists and composers whom I admire. Churchill's and President Kennedy's speeches; the album of Horowitz's appearance at the Carnegie Hall in 1959 after his long absence from public playing; the celebration of the sixtieth anniversary of Stokowski's first performance with the LSO; the farewell gala for Rudolf Bing at the Metropolitan Opera House in New York; tributes to Gerald Moore, the accompanist, on his retirement – all these in one way or another are treasured recordings.

And may I add, finally, that it gives me great satisfaction to see my own recording of Elgar's 'Cockaigne' Overture and of the Robert Mayer Children's Concert I conducted at Christmas 1973 taking their place amongst all the other records in my collection.

9 Music for everyone

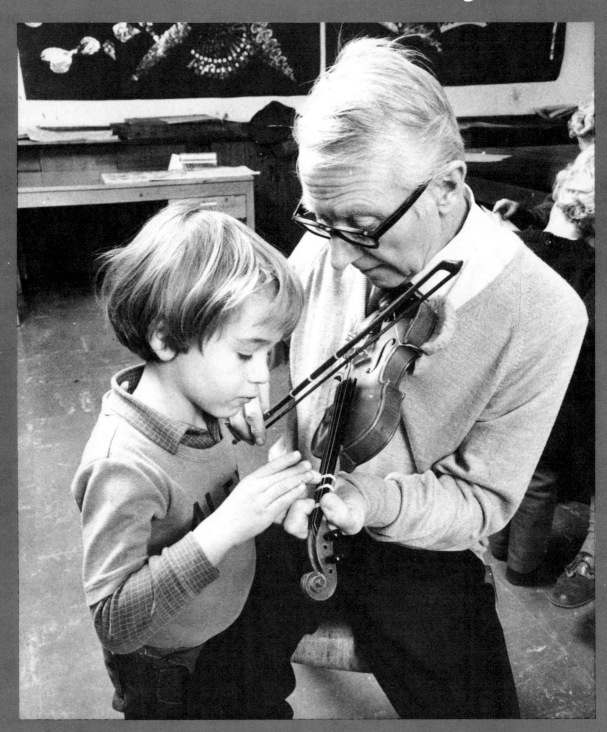

Music is all-pervasive. It permeates almost every aspect of our daily lives. Perhaps the extent to which this is so is not fully recognized because we still speak of those who are interested in music and those who are not; for while there are clearly some who are more interested than others, virtually everyone is continually encountering and responding to music in everyday life. It has become so much a part of us that we accept it for the natural thing it is and take it for granted, without needing to ask ourselves whether we are among those who *do* or those who *do not*, as far as music is concerned.

It used to be said that a few days after a new Verdi opera appeared you could hear the errand boys whistling the tunes in the street. They knew good tunes when they stumbled on them, but their whistling was not just an act of musical appreciation: in some way it made them feel better and it provided an outlet for their own emotions. Today new operas no longer have that sort of tune and the prevalent trend of popular music is rhythmic rather than melodic, while other factors such as the growth of the recording industry and the ready availability of broadcast music have produced changes in the ways we encounter and use music. But still the occasions are there when the 'non-musical' can and do actively participate. The World Cup Final at Wembley in 1966 was one of the most exciting things I have seen in my life. The excruciating tension of the extra time was almost unbearable. How stirring it was to hear the crowd on the stands at each end singing 'When the saints go marching in' more and more lustily as the tension grew. When England beat Germany the pent-up emotion was so great that there was a lump in a good many throats. This tune, although simple as music goes, is a good one, and here it met a deeply felt need to create a bond between spectators and players, to express a common purpose, support for one's side and the urge to win.

The same is true of marching songs of every army in the world. They all have the same characteristics of simplicity and unity which can be used to maintain morale and create pride of purpose. Those we used in the West in the two World Wars are well known; I have listened to thousands who sang them reliving their experiences in the Albert Hall on the eve of Remembrance Sunday and joining in as lustily as ever they did, although most of them would be the first to claim that they were not musical. So eager have armies been in the past to secure a good tune that they have sometimes stolen one another's. To many it must seem a bizarre aspect of the Second World War that troops on both sides of the conflict should have claimed possession of 'Lili Marlene'. Many of the army songs I have heard in Peking are purely Western in idiom and have been handed down from Mao Tse-tung's 'Long March', although several have been added since to reinforce the ideological position of the Chinese People's Army. The approach may be different, for the British in particular use humour as a

'Music can work its miracle on each of us if we give it a chance'

A violin lesson at Hatfield School on a Saturday morning

weapon, but in purpose there is not much to choose between 'We'll hang out the washing on the Siegfried Line' with which the British defied Hitler and 'We'll take Tiger Mountain by our stratagem' – it sounds better in Chinese – to which Chairman Mao's soldiers marched.

But to come to more solemn occasions: I never cease to be thrilled when the trumpets sound from high above the nave in Westminster Abbey for the introduction to Vaughan Williams's arrangement of 'The Old Hundredth'. And when the organ crashes into the hymn 'All people that on earth do dwell / Sing to the Lord with cheerful voice' – only to be repeated with yet greater intensity by the trumpets until people, choir, organ and brass combine in the last verse in the majesty of the doxology:

> To Father, Son, and Holy Ghost,
> The God whom heaven and earth adore,
> From men and from the angel-host
> Be praise and glory evermore

– that is one of the most glorious congregational acts of praise in Anglican music. Charles Villiers Stanford's '*Te Deum*' in B Flat, which I sang as a chorister in massed choirs in Canterbury Cathedral, holds a similar pre-eminence in my mind among church or cathedral music. For acts of praise I still long for hymns to be sung in Latin, as they were in Balliol Chapel when I was an undergraduate; '*Aeterna Christi munera*', to the tune of the same name, has a resonance and authority sung in Latin which is so often lacking in English hymnody. The Scottish metrical psalms have a rhythm of their own which makes up for some of the disadvantages of congregational singing and they are set to many of the finest tunes we possess. The old 124th has always been a favourite of mine.

> Now Israel may say and that truly,
> If that the Lord had not our cause maintained,
> If that the Lord had not our cause sustained
> When cruel men against us furiously
> Rose up in wrath to make of us their prey.

Yet it is the Welsh who are commonly supposed to have some of the best tunes, and their special choral tradition is renowned. One has only to visit an Eisteddfod to discover how high the quality of their singing can be. That this kind of music-making permeates their daily lives and is a natural response to almost every occasion, there can be no doubt. I recall one instance in the summer of 1951 when the Labour Government, with a small majority of only seven, had been hard-pressed throughout the session and in particular on the Finance Bill, which had been dragged out day after day and night after night, until we were finally on a Sitting which had lasted continuously for thirty-two hours. At 10 o'clock that night came the last vote on the Bill.

Everyone was exhausted. As Junior Whip, I went to stand by the door where the Labour Members of Parliament were being counted by my opposite number. Suddenly, as I stood there, I heard a low sound beginning to well up from the Government lobby. The doors were opened and as the Labour Members filed through the sound grew and grew. In that moment of supreme stress and strain, the Welsh Members were singing

> Guide me, O thou great Redeemer
> Pilgrim through this barren land

to the tune of '*Cwm Rhondda*', with all the passion of men and women who had reached a crucial time in their fortunes and had turned again to the childhood tunes of their Welsh valleys. As the words 'Bread of Heaven, Bread of Heaven, / Feed me till I want no more' swelled out and they burst into that wonderful harmonization of 'want no more' I felt sure it was giving them the strength to carry on the battle. It is the same fervour which invariably sweeps me away when I hear a vast congregation in St Paul's Cathedral singing with thundering organ accompaniment the 'Battle Hymn of the Republic' – 'Mine eyes have seen the glory of the coming of the Lord'.

The Americans, in their two hundred years of history, seem to have accumulated some of the most inspiring popular tunes, as well as some of the best student songs. The latter I have heard at Yale, sung by a group of students in the traditional way, sitting round the table with their beer mugs and without words or music, rather in the manner of German students in a beer cellar. British students are weak on this sort of singing; most can barely manage 'Drink to me only with thine eyes', or 'On Ilkley Moor 'baht 'at'. Nor do politicians in Britain have much to do with party songs, although I have heard tell of a Socialist Song Book. 'The Red Flag' has never been accepted by the great majority of the Labour Party as other than a perfunctory nod towards left-wing aspirations; most are hard put to it to recall the words. The Conservatives are loath to appear to take over any of our patriotic songs for political purposes. So seldom have I heard political songs outside Communist countries that I was taken aback when crossing the Baltic on my way to a European Conference at Helsinki in 1964 to find myself listening to the Danish Foreign Minister, swaying as he stood on a chair in the dining room of a rolling ship at 2 a.m., singing to the tune of 'John Brown's body':

> We'll make Nancy Astor
> Sweep the stairs of Transport House

After innumerable verses I asked his wife where he had learnt this party political doggerel. 'Oh,' she replied, 'in the early days of the Movement.' Such days seem to be past. Or is it that today political characters no longer lend themselves to this kind of musical cartoon treatment?

Film music is almost always taken for granted. When it is well done it makes its contribution to the unity of the production, but even in this subordinate role it exists as music *per se* and is absorbed into our musical consciousness. Sometimes, too, it achieves a more independent status. Arthur Bliss's music for the film of H. G. Wells's *The Shape of Things to Come* in 1935 was the first serious film score to be recognized outside the cinema. I for one was far more impressed by it than by the film itself, which in many ways I found unconvincing. Following that, the 'Warsaw' Concerto, used as the theme music for *Dangerous Moonlight*, and, among others in more recent times the haunting theme from *The Bridge over the River Kwai* or Belafonte's mesmerizing song 'Island in the Sun' have all passed into common musical language. William Walton's music for *The First of the Few*, in particular the 'Spitfire' prelude and fugue, has made a more lasting impact on me than any other film music in the last few years. He himself believes that some of the best music in this genre he has so far written was that for the film *The Battle of Britain*, which was discarded by the producers and has never yet been heard. When I was Prime Minister I was able to persuade the film company concerned to agree to return the manuscript to Walton, and I made him a present of this agreement at his seventieth birthday party at 10 Downing Street. One day I hope to hear the music performed in its own right as a suite.

So far I have only dealt with music as it appears more or less incidentally in our everyday life and on special occasions. But what has music meant to me in my home, in the concert hall or opera house? In my home it is, first and foremost, something which I make for myself, either by playing my Steinway or clavichord, or by using my record collection. Music enables me to express my moods and at the same time provides me with new experiences which refresh me spiritually and help me to continue with the daily task.

I am often asked to say who my favourite composer is, or which is my favourite piece; the truth is that there are so many composers on whom I draw for musical sustenance, and so many pieces which I love to play again and again, that the question is almost an impossible one. For me, too, so much depends on the changing mood of the moment. For instance, there are times when I want to express the sheer joy of being alive. What better than one of the early sonatas of Beethoven, Opus 10 No. 1 in C Minor, for example? Or Mozart's Sonata in A Major, No. 11 K.331, with its famous *Alla Turca* rondo for the last movement, which I played at school in a contest and which earned me the leading musical prize. Or perhaps some of Chopin's Preludes or Waltzes or Polonaises – or even one or two of the much underestimated Mendelssohn's 'Songs without Words'. Brahms's Rhapsody in E Flat, Opus 119, allows me to turn happiness into music, while

Paderewski shortly before he became Prime Minister of Poland

Schumann in his 'Carnival in Vienna' gives free expression to all the life and gaiety of the occasion, even slipping in a few bars of the 'Marseillaise', which at that time was forbidden music.

In more reflective mood, and feeling the need for peaceful reconciliation with myself after a day of conflict, I turn to Bach, the Preludes and Fugues, or perhaps Harriet Cohen's piano arrangement of '*Liebster Jesu, wir sind hier*', and Walter Rummel's of '*Ertödt uns durch dein güte*', or the slow movements of Beethoven's sonatas. Schubert's 'Posthumous' Sonata in B Flat, or the last movement of Beethoven's last sonata, No. 111 in C Minor, all bring me particular solace, as does Brahms's simple Intermezzo in E Flat Major, Opus 117.

Nor should Schumann's miniatures like the '*Kinderscenen*' be underestimated. '*Träumerei*' – 'Dreaming' – has a marvellous simplicity, which it is unfortunately more difficult to do justice to than many a technically fiendish piece. At his concert at Carnegie Hall – his first public appearance for twelve years – Horowitz played this as one of his encores. He had recorded it in the thirties, but his performance that night showed that the man with the greatest pianistic technique since Busoni had also such supreme control that he could play '*Träumerei*', without affectation or false emphasis and allow it to speak for itself, even better than he had been able to do twenty years before. Whatever my mood, there is something on the piano to meet it.

But these are private occasions. Much of the music we enjoy is in public, in the concert hall or in the opera house. Let us approach this with the attitude that at least there will always be something of interest in a performance, and in all probability much that we can enjoy. Just occasionally there will be a performance which will remain in the memory beyond all others and which we shall be thankful not to have missed. Sometimes it will be because of the atmosphere, on other occasions because of the personalities. Sometimes because the music excels, sometimes – the rarest moments of all – when all three coalesce in a breathtaking beauty.

The memories flood back; Sir Thomas Beecham, at one of his last concerts, conducting in a chair at the Festival Hall, with Cherniavsky playing Saint-Saëns's first Cello Concerto in A Minor, the old man's and the young cellist's heads so close together they seemed almost to be communing over the music rather than presenting a performance; Josef Krips happily wending his way through a sublime performance of Beethoven's 'Pastoral' Symphony, placid, unhurried and unhurrying, at one with nature, as Beethoven meant it to be; Herbert von Karajan, with the Vienna Philharmonic Orchestra, playing Richard Strauss's '*Also sprach Zarathustra*', the opening C Minor/B Major dissonance developing through the wild waltz until all is reconciled in the quiet closing chords of C Major – so stupendous was the applause that von Karajan picked up his baton for an encore, something I have

With the Queen Mother, Sir Arthur Bliss (left), Sir Robert Mayer (centre) and Sir Malcolm Sargent (right) at the LSO Gala Concert in 1964

never known him do at any other time, and to our astonishment, and to the disgust of the Austrian Ambassador, who immediately walked out, broke into the sounds of Johann Strauss's 'Tales from the Vienna Woods'; many, many performances by Artur Rubinstein, the Beethoven, Chopin, Brahms, Saint-Saëns Concertos, and then the generosity of his encores, very often the resounding Polonaise in A Flat of Chopin; the Bach Choir, on a Sunday before Easter, singing the *St Matthew Passion*, half before lunch and half afterwards – and on one occasion the soprano being taken ill just after the beginning of her first aria, when quick as a flash David Willcocks, the conductor, brought in all the sopranos to sing the rest of the aria from sight; Cantelli, fated to be killed in an air crash so early in his life, who seemed more likely than anyone to follow Toscanini, producing brilliant performances, warm and not hard; Stravinsky conducting 'The Firebird' at the end of his last concert in London, his arms dropping lower and lower as he completed the suite – we thought he would never manage it, but in the last few moments he suddenly recovered his strength and brought it to its triumphant

conclusion; afterwards he signed for me three sketches of himself conducting, writing on them, 'Not bad at all!'

The concert I remember that excelled all others took place in the Albert Hall on 28 September 1963. To begin with it was imprinted on my memory because it started at 9.15 p.m. – late for a concert in the post-war years. I went because three violinists, Yehudi Menuhin and the Oistrakhs, father and son, were playing, taking it turn and turn about to play together or to conduct. That night, with the Moscow Philharmonic Orchestra conducted by David Oistrakh, Yehudi Menuhin played Beethoven's Violin Concerto in D. I have long admired him as a man for his wide and varied interests, as well as for his playing. We have written to each other innumerable letters about the problems of the world and the future of mankind. That night at the Albert Hall it seemed at times as though his concern with these matters was inspiring his playing; he produced such purity of tone, such breadth of style and such a depth of interpretation that I was transported beyond the surroundings of the concert hall into another world; I doubt whether I shall ever hear Beethoven's Violin Concerto played in the same way again. It was an experience not just for that evening but one which will remain with me for the rest of my life, for in Menuhin's hands the music became a profound embodiment of human values.

Only on rare occasions will a combination of circumstances make such performances possible; nevertheless, they represent something towards which every musician should aspire. Many of the conditions necessary for this pursuit of excellence may, in themselves, appear to be run-of-the-mill, humdrum matters: at what age children should start to learn how to play instruments; how their general education should be combined with specialization in music; how the performer may avoid the tensions of insecurity, yet, at the same time, be spurred on to ever greater artistry. But this is true of all human affairs. We no longer accept that the impoverished garret is the *sine qua non* of artistic endeavour. The place of the artist in society is now well recognized. It rests with artists themselves to ensure that neither their creative urge nor their keenness in performance is blunted by the distractions of our material world.

The written word and the spoken word tell their own story. But, while a picture can be adequately described to those who know the world around them without their actually seeing it, there is a limit to what words can achieve in describing musical perfection. The structure, the instrumentation, the history, the purpose, the life of the composer and the executant – all these can be put into words; but at this point words exhaust their usefulness. There is nothing further they can do. The music remains. It is only the music which can then work its miracle on each of us, if we give it the chance. For all who give it their feeling and understanding, music will remain a joy for ever.

Glossary

Music is an art-form and the expressions used when talking about music cannot always be defined in absolute terms. In many cases a word can have more than one meaning or be interpreted by musicians in different ways. The explanations given in this glossary are those in popular use and are, in some instances, an over-simplification of a complex concept. Anyone wishing to extend their understanding of the terminology in use among musicians should consult *Grove's Dictionary of Music and Musicians* (9 volumes) 5th edition 1954, published by Macmillan Ltd and available in the reference section of most public libraries.

Adagio From the Italian, meaning 'leisurely'. A slow, often poetic and tuneful piece of music.

Allegretto Not as gay or brisk as 'Allegro' but not as slow as 'Andante'.

Allegro From the Italian, meaning 'cheerful'. A brisk or lively tempo.

Alto From the Italian, meaning 'high'. An unusually high adult male voice. Also the lowest boys' or women's (contralto) range.

Andante From the Italian, meaning 'going'. A flowing, moderate tempo.

Aria A solo song, often consisting of three distinct parts, in a major musical work.

Arpeggio 'Harp-like'. A chord of three or more notes played in rapid succession, normally starting with the lowest note.

Arrangement The re-writing of a piece of music for a specific purpose, usually altering the instruments for which it was originally composed. For example, a piano solo could be arranged or translated into an orchestral piece or vice versa.

Atonal Not in any key (see also 'Harmony').

Augmented A chord in which the tone interval is increased by one half-tone.

Bar The division of a piece of music into groups (measures) of beats.

Bar-line The vertical line drawn across the horizontal lines (staff) on a sheet of music.

Baritone The adult male singing range lying between tenor and bass.

Bass (*a*) The lowest adult male singing range. (*b*) The lowest lines or lowest notes or 'voice' in a piece of music.

Brass Wind instruments made of brass, familiar from the popular brass bands. Trumpets, trombones, tubas and French horns are part of the brass section of an orchestra.

Bravura From the Italian meaning 'courage.' A term used to indicate that the music should be performed in such a way as to display the brilliance of the instrument and of the performer.

Canon A composition for several voices (or instruments) in which the melody or theme is successively and identically imitated or repeated by each voice starting at a given interval after the other voice or voices. For example the well-known song 'Frère Jacques'.

Cembalo The shortened name for the clavicembalo, better known as the harpsichord.

Chamber music Literally, music for private enjoyment. In the seventeenth century, music which was written for use other than the church or the theatre. (There were then no public orchestral concerts.) Today the term is applied to any music performed by a small group of musicians without a conductor.

Chamber orchestra A small-scale orchestra.

Chorale A short composition, often of a religious nature, designed to be sung by a choir with or without organ or orchestral accompaniment. Historically the chorale is the origin of the church hymn.

Chord Two or more different notes played simultaneously by one instrument (a harp or keyboard instrument) or by a group of single-note instruments.

Chorus (*a*) The vocal equivalent to an orchestra, consisting of groups of sopranos, altos, tenors and basses. (*b*) The recurring melody or theme following the verses or stanzas of a song.

Clavichord A stringed keyboard instrument dating from the fifteenth century. Although of limited range and volume it is capable of very wide and delicate variation in tone; the strings are struck, and the note is created by a brass tangent which both sounds and stops the strings.

Concerto The meaning of this word has changed during the course of musical history. (*a*) Formerly it described a work for an orchestra or group of players, with or without solo

instruments, e.g. Bach: Brandenburg Concertos. (*b*) In the nineteenth century it usually meant a work for one or more virtuosic solo instruments with orchestral accompaniment, e.g. Grieg: Piano Concerto (piano and orchestra). (*c*) In the twentieth century both (*a*) and (*b*) are in use, e.g. (*a*) Stravinsky: Dumbarton Oaks Concerto; (*b*) Vaughan Williams: Tuba Concerto. Some composers have made the orchestra itself fulfil the role of the virtuoso, e.g. Bartok: Concerto for Orchestra.

Con molta espressione From the Italian, meaning 'with much expression'.

Console (**organ**) That part of an organ which houses the keys, manuals, pedals, stops and other controls.

Counterpoint A form of musical composition where the melody is accompanied by another melody and the interest is centred on the structure and interweaving of the melodic lines.

Crochet (**quarter note**) Name given to a note whose 'value' is one time-beat in a 4/4 bar (four beats in a bar).

Damping pedal (**piano**) Often known as the 'soft' pedal. One of the two conventional pedals of a piano which has the effect of reducing or damping the volume of sound when a string is struck by the hammer. This is achieved either by moving the hammers closer to the strings (upright pianos), thus shortening the strike distance, or by shifting the hammers sideways (grand pianos) so that they strike only one or two of the two or three strings each note requires.

Desk The name given to the seat and music stand of a member of an orchestra.

Diminished chord A chord in which the tone interval is decreased by one half-tone; for example a diminished third has an interval of only two and a half tones.

Divertimento From the Italian, meaning 'an amusement'. A not too serious work in several movements, usually for a small instrumental group.

Dotted rhythm Could also be popularly called a syncopated rhythm. Any note which on the score is followed by a full-stop, i.e. a dot, is increased by half its time value. For example a dotted crotchet is worth three quavers. As the number of beats in any given bar is fixed, this results in a break in the rhythm or sequence of beats.

Ensemble From the French, meaning 'together'. A small group of musicians playing together with perfect understanding. It is a term frequently used as an aid to describing the quality of a specific performance, e.g. 'The ensemble was bad, very ragged with several false entries.'

Fifths See 'Thirds'. The tone interval is five whole tones.

Finale From the Italian, meaning 'the ending'. The last movement or section of a piece of music.

First-time bar A convenient term used to refer to the bar or bars at the end of a section of music which is to be repeated. The first-time bar is only played at the first playing but, for musical-technical reasons, is replaced by other bars or omitted altogether at the second playing.

Flautist A flute player.

Fourths See 'Thirds'. The tone interval is four whole tones.

Fugue From the Italian *fuga*, meaning 'flight'. A contrapuntal composition in which a single-line theme, the subject, is introduced and, often in a strictly mathematical manner, is taken up by one or two or more 'voices' (parts) entering successively with subject and answer in such a manner as to produce a harmonious whole. Unlike a canon, the subject can be accompanied by notes other than the 'subject' and the subject theme can be reversed, inverted or decorated.

Harmony (*a*) The combining of sounds to make a chord. (*b*) The theory of music concerned with the correct progression of notes and chords. (*c*) The relationship between chords and their progression. (*d*) Tonal harmony: the theory which dominates many forms of musical composition in that any theme or tune and the chords accompanying it have a tonal relationship built upon the tonal base, or key-centre, and other tones derived from this base. Harmony governs this relationship. (*e*) Atonal harmony: in contrast to tonality, atonality uses harmonic progressions consisting of chords which are not in any key and give no impression of being related to a key-centre.

Harpsichord The English name for the clavicembalo or cembalo. A seventeenth-century keyboard instrument in which the strings are plucked and not struck. It is the only keyboard string instrument to have two manuals or keyboards and a number of stops which can alter the nature of the sound made when a key is struck. The sound volume produced is fixed and it is not possible to alter the volume of an individual note.

Intervals The term used to describe the tone 'distance' between two notes. Intervals are named after the number of tones separating them – thirds, fourths and the like.

Key (*a*) A succession or scale of tones bearing a fixed relationship to each other and based on a specific note or tone called the key-note or tonal base. The key is called after the key-note, i.e. the key of C is based on the note C and so on. There are minor and major keys. Regrettably the terms 'major' and 'minor' defy neat definition; by common consent a major chord and key sounds gay, and a minor, sad. (*b*) The black and white ivory and ebony levers which are struck when playing a keyboard instrument. (*c*) The levers that operate the valves or sound-holes of wind instruments.

Keyboard The array of white and black keys with which a keyboard instrument is played.

Keyboard instrument A stringed instrument or a wind instrument played by means of a keyboard and characterized by the fact that more than one note can be played at a time. The piano, organ, harpsichord, clavichord, and spinet are keyboard instruments. A harp, however, is not, as it is played like a guitar, by the fingers plucking the tuned strings.

K. number A convenient abbreviation for 'Köchel Verzeichnis', the catalogue number assigned in 1862 by Dr Ludwig Ritter von Köchel (1800–1877) to the complete index of all Wolfgang Amadeus Mozart's compositions. (Mozart did not assign Opus numbers to his compositions.) Thus his Piano Concerto in C Minor is referred to as K.491.

Largo From the Italian, meaning 'broad' or 'slow'. A measured, stately rhythm.

Leader The occupant of the first desk of the first violins, the leading group of violins in an orchestra. The Leader of an orchestra is responsible for rehearsing the orchestra in the absence of the conductor. He or she is often a soloist in his or her own right. Musically, the Leader is the senior member of an orchestra.

Lento From the Italian, meaning 'slow'.

Leitmotif From the German, meaning 'leading theme'. A phrase used when discussing a basic theme or tune which is repeatedly used in various forms and can be dominant throughout a major musical work. A *leitmotif* is used to denote specific characters or objects in opera or in descriptive, so called programme, music. The term was not used before the time of Wagner, i.e. not before the end of the nineteenth century.

Lieder (singular – **Lied**) From the German meaning 'songs', pronounced 'leader'. A serious musical setting of a poem for solo voice and piano

accompaniment, commonly applied to the songs of Schubert, Schumann and Hugo Wolf.

Madrigal An unaccompanied vocal setting for four or five voices of a poem. The origin of the word is much disputed but has been in use since the early fourteenth century.

Manual (organ) Any one of the two or more keyboards of an organ.

Metronome A clockwork or electronic instrument producing an audible tick or click and whose speed can be adjusted. It is calibrated in beats per minute and is often used as a practice aid.

Minuet A short, stately dance piece in triple time (three beats to a bar). Traditionally it consists of three parts, the first and third being identical or similar, while the middle part is in a contrasting mood or key.

Motet A short, usually religious, work for unaccompanied voices. The form is customarily polyphonic. In the classical motet the words as well as the music undergo progressive changes with each additional voice. The composition of motets reached its height in the sixteenth century.

Movement A symphony (orchestra), concerto (orchestra and soloist), or sonata (soloist) is divided into movements, usually three, four or five in number, in differing tempos and related keys.

Nobilemente From the Italian, meaning 'nobly'. An instruction qualifying the tempo marking indicating that the piece should be played in a stately manner.

Obbligato An indispensable (as compared with an optional) solo performance during a movement of an orchestral piece. In the case of a concerto the *obbligato* is designed to demonstrate the virtuosity of the soloist and/or the instrument. In choral works an aria will occasionally have an instrumental *obbligato* accompanying the singer as a subordinate soloist.

Opus (Op.) number From the Latin, meaning 'work'. The method used by composers (or sometimes by editors and publishers of music) to identify a composition. The number, starting from 1 for the first composed or published work, can also be applied to a group of compositions belonging to a particular period or phase in the composer's life, or to a number of similar pieces; the individual compositions within the group then receive a second number, for example Beethoven's famous 'Moonlight' Sonata is Op. 27 No. 2.

Orchestral colour (*a*) The sound of an orchestra which is determined by the number of instruments, the balance between various groups of instruments and the presence or absence of certain instruments. The acoustics of the performance hall will also have considerable effect on orchestral colour. (*b*) The effect of the quality and character of the playing.

Ornaments Decorative notes forming an embellishment around the principal note. Ornaments can take the form of trills (a rapid alternation between the main note and a note a half or a whole tone higher), turns (one note above and one note below the main note which is played twice, once in the middle and once at the end of the turn), mordants (two or four-note trills), or *appoggiatura* (a single note slurred on to the main note).

Part-song A vocal composition for several parts (voices), as distinct from a solo or unison song.

Percussion The group of orchestral instruments which are struck rather than blown or bowed. The timpani or kettle drums, side (snare) drum, bass drum, cymbals and triangle are the usual percussion instruments of a symphony orchestra. The percussionist may however be called upon to perform on any of a large array of occasional instruments such as cuckoo whistles, sirens, tubular bells, sleigh bells, tambourines or maraccas.

Philharmonic (orchestra or society) From the Greek meaning 'loving harmony'. Originally used for the naming of clubs or societies with the common interest of classical, as opposed to popular, music. It has since been adopted by a number of leading symphony orchestras and may often indicate that the orchestra is supported by subscriptions from members of their philharmonic society.

Piano From the Italian meaning 'softly'. The opposite of '*forte*', meaning 'loud'. Hence the correct name for the piano, the pianoforte, the first instrument of the string keyboard family capable of being played both loudly and softly. This was achieved through a complicated and sophisticated system of levers and springs, known as the 'action', which operated the striking, felt-covered, hammers.

Piano trio/quartet A composition for piano and two or three other instruments – usually strings – in which all the instruments are of equal thematic and musical importance. The term is also used to describe the ensemble performing this type of work.

Pizzicato From the Italian, meaning 'plucked'. It is an instruction to violins, violas, cellos or double basses to play a note or notes by plucking the string with a finger rather than playing it with the bow.

Plainsong A medieval form of vocal composition (usually religious) which is sung in unison and unaccompanied. It is characterized by its free rhythm, which is closely linked to the natural enunciation of the spoken voice. Its final form, Gregorian Chant, survives in Roman Catholic church music.

Polyphonic A form of composition where the voices or instruments each have their own 'line' or melody as contrasted with the more familiar form where the instruments or voices accompany one melody.

Prelude A short, introductory piece of music which is followed by the main work. More familiarly, it is simply a short imaginative composition, standing on its own or in groups of similar pieces.

Presto From the Italian, meaning 'fast'.

Quaver The name given to a note whose 'value' is half of a crotchet.

Register (*a*) An aspect of the tonal range of an instrument. (*b*) The change in *timbre* or quality of the human or organ voice that occurs as it progresses up or down the scale, e.g. chest register, head register. (*c*) On the organ, a set of pipes of similar tonal quality; the name of the register is written on the stop which brings that set of pipes into operation. Registers are called after the sound they imitate – *vox humana* (the human voice), trumpet, and the like.

Rondo From the Italian, meaning 'round'. A piece of music where the original theme or tune is repeated in the original key but the repetition is usually preceded by a linking or related section known as an 'episode'.

Scherzo From the Italian, meaning 'humorous'. A lively, entertaining and usually short piece or movement of a composition.

Score The musical text (the equivalent of the 'book' of a play) containing, vertically aligned below each other, the complete notation for each instrument or groups of instruments so that all can be read simultaneously. It is customary to 'score' instruments of the highest pitch at the top of the page and other instruments in descending order of pitch. Traditionally, however, the strings are grouped together below the percussion instruments. In the case of a concerto, the solo instrument occupies the lines of the score between the strings and the percussion. The 'full' score is used by the conductor and by students and occasionally by the soloist during rehearsals. For study purposes most orchestral works are available as 'miniature' scores photographically reduced from the full score.

Sforzando From the Italian, meaning 'forced'. An instruction, usually indicated by the letters 'sf' or a 'v' against the notes concerned, instructing the performer that those notes or chords should be played sharply and loudly, in contrast with the other notes of the passage.

Sinfonia, sinfonietta (orchestra) From the Italian meaning 'symphony', 'little symphony'. These are terms that have come to be applied to small, often specialized orchestras which would not normally have a full complement of percussion, brass and woodwind instruments.

Sonata From the Italian, meaning 'a piece sounded' (distinguishing it from 'cantata', a piece sung). A composition for one or two instruments usually consisting of several related movements.

Soprano The adult female's normal upper singing range.

String trio/quartet A composition for three or four string instruments, for example, violin, viola and cello. Also used to describe the group of musicians performing such compositions.

Strings The bowed string instruments – in the case of an orchestra these would normally consist of violins, violas, cellos and double basses.

Stop (instrumental) (*a*) Stringed instruments: the action of placing a finger on the string to produce a required note. (*b*) Horn-playing: to alter the pitch and quality of a note by placing the hand in the bell of the instrument.

Stops (organ) The manual controls (switches or pistons) which are used to alter the tone and character of the notes produced by one or more of the keyboards (manuals) by introducing or changing the 'register'.

Sustaining pedal (piano) One of the two customary pedals of the piano which lifts the dampers away from the strings and allows a note or notes to continue sounding after the key has been released. Also known (wrongly) as the 'loud' pedal.

Suite A group of three or more, often related, instrumental pieces in various tempi and rhythms.

Swell box (organ) The mechanism by means of which the volume of sound can be increased or decreased. It is normally operated by means of a swivel pedal, rather like the accelerator in a motor car, by the right foot. For technical reasons, the sound volume of an individual organ note cannot be individually controlled; consequently groups of pipes fed from a common air reserve (the swell box) have their air flow and volume controlled by means of a device reminiscent of venetian blinds which are opened and closed by the swell pedal. Not all manuals are connected to a swell box.

Symphony A major musical composition for a full orchestra, in two or more parts or movements in a related key. Hence the term a 'symphony orchestra', comprising all customary instruments.

Tempo From the Italian, meaning 'speed'. The speed at which a piece of music should be or is performed. This is indicated by the composer either by means of a designation such as *allegro*, *andante* and the like or by means of a metronome mark which gives the number of beats per minute.

Tenor A male voice with the highest conventional adult male range. The term is also applied to certain wind instruments which are available in different ranges – e.g. the saxophone.

Timbre A term used to describe the quality of sound of an instrument or group of instruments. In many ways it is a synonym for 'colour' but it implies a more tangible attribute.

Time The fundamental rhythm or beat of any piece of music, customarily indicated in various ways which imply the number of beats in a bar. It is spoken of, for example, as 2-time (two beats as, for example, in the polka or jig), 3/4-time (three beats in a bar as in a waltz), 4/4-time (four beats in a bar as in a simple jazz tune). There are many variations to this system, not all of which are based on the fundamental concept of four beats to a bar and fractions thereof. Other aspects of the very general expression 'time' are accent, metre (the pacing of accents) and tempo.

Timpani (singular – **timpanum**) Tuned kettle drums. In modern timpani the note can be altered quickly by changing the tension in the skin by means of a foot pedal. Timpani are the principal percussion instruments of the concert orchestra which are played by the 'timpanist'. The familiar 'V' signature to war-time overseas news broadcasts was played on timpani.

Thirds A two-note chord where the two notes are three whole tones apart. In contrast to fourths and fifths, a third sounds pleasant whereas the other two are 'empty'. It is the customary interval for two people singing in 'close harmony'.

Tonic The first degree (key-note) of the scale, e.g. D in the keys of D major and D minor.

Touch (piano) The highly personal and individualistic tone imparted by a pianist to his instrument by means of the infinite variations of technique which are all involved in the action

of striking and releasing a note or a succession of notes. It is a subject of considerable argument; scientific measurements have been unable to detect the difference between individual pianists and a machine striking the keys, yet the listener is aware of an identifiable difference.

Transposition Changing or rewriting or 'translating' a piece of music from one key into another. This is done to either raise or lower the range to suit, for example, a singer, or to suit an instrument other than the one for which the music was originally written. When the key is changed by the composer in the course of a composition or movement, this is called a 'modulation', not a 'transposition', the key being changed through a succession of related harmonies so as not to be abrupt and unsettling. Certain wind instruments (e.g. the clarinet) which, for technical reasons, are constructed on the basis of a key other than C, are known as transposing instruments as their music is written in one key but the instrument produces a sound in another key.

Treble (*a*) The highest of a boy's singing range, the male equivalent to the female soprano. (*b*) Treble is also the name given to the upper line of piano music and other instrumental music which lies in the upper half of the normal musical range. It is indicated by the 'treble clef', which is a stylized letter 'G' whose centre rests on the line occupied by the note 'G'.

Trill A decoration to a note consisting of a rapid, rhythmic alternation with the note immediately higher. See also 'Ornaments'.

Variations A form of musical composition for one or more instruments, or for an orchestra, which opens with a short and often traditional tune which is subsequently elaborated and re-arranged in a series of short 'variations' or pieces, all based on the original theme.

Vivace From the Italian, meaning 'lively'. Used as a qualification of other tempo instructions, for example '*allegro vivace*', indicating a more lively tempo than '*allegro*'.

Voluntary An organ solo played either before or after the church service. The voluntary is not part of the religious office.

Woodwind The origin of the term is to be found in the fact that this group of instruments, in contrast to the brass, was made of wood. The 'official' name of the bassoon, for example, is '*fagotti*', meaning a bundle of sticks, which it not only resembled but from which it was also made. The woodwind family includes the oboe, clarinet and bassoon, whose sound is made by a vibrating reed, and the flute and the piccolo which do not use a reed.

Biographical notes on composers

Arnold, Malcolm (b. 1921) English composer and formerly principal trumpet with the London Philharmonic Orchestra. His work includes ballets, film scores, overtures, concertos (including one for the harmonica), six symphonies and a toy symphony.

Bach, Johann Sebastian (1685–1750) German composer and organist. Although he was famous among his contemporaries for his playing of the organ, clavichord and harpsichord, his compositions were little considered until the nineteenth century. For twenty-seven years he was cantor of St Thomas's Church, Leipzig; hence his large volume of church compositions, many for specific occasions, e.g. the *St John* and *St Matthew Passions*, the *Christmas* and *Easter Oratorios*. The remainder of his work includes compositions for the organ, such as his preludes and fugues, and for the harpsichord, clavichord, violin and orchestra.

Balfe, Michael (1808–1870) Irish operatic singer and composer; sang, managed and composed opera all his working life. Only one of his operas, *The Bohemian Girl*, survives.

Bax, Sir Arnold (1883–1953) English composer of chamber, orchestral and choral music, much influenced by Irish literature and myth. Master of the King's Music from 1942 until his death.

Beethoven, Ludwig van (1770–1827) German composer and pianist; he worked at the court in Bonn until he was twenty-two when he settled in Vienna. He studied briefly with Mozart and Haydn. He developed and enriched the forms of symphony, sonata and piano concerto and is considered to be the bridge between classical and Romantic music. He wrote nine symphonies, including the 'Eroica', five piano concertos, including the 'Emperor', thirty-two piano sonatas, among them the 'Moonlight' Sonata. He wrote one opera, *Fidelio*, and two masses. His work also includes theatre music, violin sonatas, piano solos and string trios, quartets and quintets.

Bellini, Vincenzo (1801–1835) Italian opera composer. His operas include *The Puritans*, *Norma* and *Capulets and Montagus*.

Bennett, Richard Rodney (b. 1936) English composer. Has written operas for Covent Garden and the English Opera Company and much film music, as well as chamber and orchestral works.

Bennett, Sir William Sterndale (1816–1875) English pianist and composer, befriended by Mendelssohn. He held many teaching and academic posts; his small repertoire of compositions consisted mainly of piano works.

Berlioz, Hector (1803–1869) French composer at the hub of nineteenth-century Romanticism, a pioneer of modern orchestration. His works were often musical expressions of literary themes, for example his overtures 'Waverley', 'King Lear', 'Harold in Italy'.

Bernstein, Leonard (b. 1918) American conductor, pianist and composer. His work, which includes symphonies, an opera, musicals and religious pieces, often shows the influence of jazz.

Bizet, Georges (1838–1875) French composer, mostly of operas, his most famous being *Carmen*, which was first performed just before his death. His incidental music to Alphonse Daudet's play *L'Arlésienne* is also well known.

Bliss, Sir Arthur (1891–1975) English composer; his early works were often for unusual combinations of instruments and voices. His compositions include the 'Colour' Symphony, the choral-orchestral work 'Morning Heroes', the ballet 'Checkmate' and the film score for H. G. Wells's *Things to Come*. Master of the Queen's Music from 1953 until his death.

Boccherini, Luigi (1743–1805) Italian composer and cellist. He wrote much chamber music, mainly string quartets and quintets, as well as four concertos for cello.

Brahms, Johannes (1833–1897) German composer. Wrote Romantic music using classical forms. Nineteenth-century critics grouped themselves behind Brahms or his opposite, Wagner. Amongst his works are four symphonies, two piano concertos, a violin concerto and a double concerto for violin and cello, as well as chamber music, songs and choral-orchestral compositions.

Britten, Benjamin (b. 1913) English composer, pianist and conductor; artistic director and founder (with Peter Pears and Eric Crozier) of the Aldeburgh Festival. He has written many operas and operettas including *Noyes Fludde*, *Peter Grimes*, *Billy Budd* and *Gloriana*, as well as choral and orchestral works, chamber music and song cycles. His works for children 'Let's Make an Opera' and 'A Young Person's Guide to the Orchestra' are also well known.

Bruckner, Anton (1824–1896) Austrian composer and organist; he did not devote himself to composition until his forties. He wrote Romantic music and was influenced by Wagner. His works include nine symphonies, four masses, a string quintet and a *Te Deum*.

Castelnuovo-Tedesco, Mario (1895–1968) Italian-born composer who later settled in America. His work includes choral music, opera, piano and violin concertos and music for the synagogue.

Chaminade, Cécile (1857–1944) French composer and pianist. Although mainly known for her piano pieces she also wrote a ballet, a comic opera, songs and orchestral suites.

Chopin, Frédéric (1810–1849) Half French, half Polish composer and pianist, who lived mostly in Paris; grouped with Schumann and Mendelssohn as a Romantic. His work, written almost entirely for the piano, was uniquely expressive. It included twenty-seven études, twenty-five preludes, nineteen nocturnes, three sonatas, fifty-five mazurkas and two concertos.

Debussy, Claude (1862–1918) French composer and founder of what is termed the 'Impressionist' school in music, which tended to avoid drama, formality, convention and narrative. Among his most famous works are the opera *Pelléas and Mélisande*, the piano preludes and the orchestral pieces 'Nocturnes', 'La Mer' and 'L'Apres-midi d'un faune'.

Delibes, Léo (1836–1891) French composer and organist principally known for his ballets, such as 'Coppélia'. He also wrote songs, operas and masses.

Delius, Frederick (1862–1934) English composer of German descent. His work, which gained acceptance in Britain largely through the enthusiasm of Sir Thomas Beecham, includes operas, orchestral variations, rhapsodies, concertos for piano, violin and cello, choral works, chamber music and songs.

Donizetti, Gaetano (1797–1848) Italian composer of more than sixty operas, among them *Lucia di Lammermoor* and *Don Pasquale*.

Dvořák, Antonín (1841–1904) Czech composer who began his career as a viola player in the Prague National Theatre. Brahms gave him encouragement as a composer and from the mid-1870s onwards his work became increasingly popular, both in his own country and abroad. For three years he was principal of the National Conservatory in New York, a stay which resulted in his famous 'New World' Symphony. He was one of the leaders of the nationalist movement in music and made great use in his compositions of the folk idioms of Czechoslovakia.

Elgar, Sir Edward (1857–1934) English composer who also began as a professional musician. It was largely through the Three Choirs Festival, with which he was much associated, that he first became known as a composer, and his 'Enigma Variations', written at the age of forty-two, established him in the front rank. Other well-known works include *The Dream of Gerontius*, the oratorios *The Apostles* and *The Kingdom*, the 'Cockaigne' Overture and the 'Pomp and Circumstance' marches. He was appointed Master of the King's Music in 1924.

Franck, César (1822–1890) Belgian-French composer and organist. Although a successful organist and teacher – he became organ professor at the Paris Conservatoire in 1872 – he was recognized as a composer only late in life. He wrote much music for the piano, as well as oratorios, symphonic poems and a symphony.

Goss, Sir John (1800–1880) British composer and organist at St Paul's Cathedral. Composed mainly church music.

Gounod, Charles François (1818–1893) French composer and organist. His most famous work is the opera *Faust*; he also composed church music, oratorios, devout songs and masses.

Grieg, Edvard (1843–1907) Norwegian composer of Scottish descent. Like Dvořák he was a nationalist and based much of his music on Norwegian folk tunes. At Ibsen's request he wrote the incidental music for *Peer Gynt*; his other compositions included choral works, a piano concerto, violin sonatas and songs.

Guilmant, Félix (1837–1911) French composer and organist at the Church of the Trinity in Paris. Travelled widely giving organ recitals and taught many organists of the succeeding generation. Composed principally for the organ, also reviving earlier works for the instrument.

Handel, George Frederic (1685–1759) German-born composer who later became a British subject; also noted as a harpsichordist and organist. As well as composing over forty Italian operas for Covent Garden Theatre and the King's Theatre, he was the first to use the biblical oratorio form; he wrote over twenty works in this idiom, the most famous being the *Messiah*. His orchestral music includes the 'Water Music' and 'Fireworks Music'.

Haydn, Joseph (1732–1809) Austrian composer. As a boy he sang in the cathedral choir in Vienna and later became Kapellmeister to the Esterhazy family. He established the accepted forms of the symphony and string quartet. Under the influence of Handel he wrote several oratorios and more than twenty operas; he also composed the Austrian national anthem.

Henze, Hans Werner (b. 1926) German composer best known for his operas and ballet scores such as 'Ondine'. He has also written 'Dance Marathon' for jazz band and symphony orchestra, cantatas and other choral and orchestral music.

Howells, Herbert (b. 1892) English composer, teacher and former cathedral organist. His work, mainly church music, includes choral settings of religious texts.

Hummel, Johann (1778–1837) Austrian composer, pianist and teacher, a pupil of Mozart. Wrote many works for the piano as well as opera and church music.

Humperdinck, Engelbert (1854–1921) German composer, a friend of Wagner at Bayreuth. His opera *Hansel and Gretel* was his greatest success; he also wrote others on fairytale themes.

Ives, Charles (1874–1954) American composer. A radical innovator who spent much of his life working for an insurance company in New York, composing in his spare time. His compositions, which include symphonies, choral works and chamber music, often allow for improvisation by the performers.

Janáček, Leoš (1854–1928) Czech composer and choral conductor. Study of his native folk songs and speech was a prime influence on his work, which includes operas such as *The Cunning Little Vixen* and *Katya Kabanova*, choral and orchestral compositions, song cycles and folk song arrangements.

Lambert, Constant (1905–1951) English composer, conductor and writer on music. Particularly involved in ballet; he wrote ballets for Diaghilev in the late 1920s and was Musical Director of the Old Vic-Sadlers Wells. His best-known work, 'The Rio Grande' for chorus, piano and orchestra, is much influenced by jazz.

Leighton, Kenneth (b. 1929) English composer, teacher and pianist. Works include a cello concerto, a violin concerto and one for viola.

Liszt, Franz (1811–1886) Hungarian composer and pianist, during his early life an immensely successful performer. He later took holy orders and was known as the Abbé Liszt. His best compositions are his works for piano, including the Hungarian Rhapsodies, based on gipsy music, his orchestral pieces and his songs.

MacDowell, Edward (1861–1908) American composer and pianist. Encouraged by Liszt he first gained a reputation in Germany. His works include symphonic poems, orchestral suites, the 'Indian Suite' among them, piano concertos and four piano sonatas.

Mahler, Gustav (1860–1911) Austrian composer and conductor. He conducted the Austrian State Opera for ten years, and in America the Metropolitan Opera and the Philharmonic Orchestra. His work includes nine symphonies, a tenth unfinished, some of these including voice solos and chorus; he also wrote song-cycles, for example 'Song of the Earth', 'Songs of a Wayfarer' and 'Songs on the Death of Children'. His method of composition is considered to be the forerunner of Schoenberg's twelve-tone technique.

Martin, George Clement (1844–1916) English ecclesiastical composer and organist who succeeded Stainer at St Paul's Cathedral. Most notable among his compositions was the *Te Deum* sung on the steps of St Paul's for Queen Victoria's Diamond Jubilee.

Massenet, Jules (1842–1912) French composer who produced many stage works – operas, incidental music and a lyric play – besides overtures, a piano concerto, cantatas and oratorios.

Mendelssohn, Felix (1809–1847) German conductor, pianist and Romantic composer; a friend of Goethe and Weber. He was a leader in the Bach revival and the first person to conduct the *St Matthew Passion* after the death of the composer. He wrote important works in all the musical forms except opera, and was one of the first to write independent concert overtures such as 'Fingal's Cave'.

Mozart, Wolfgang Amadeus (1756–1791) Austrian composer who came from a family of musicians. As a child prodigy he toured Europe with his father and sister playing the harpsichord. He composed over six hundred works, including operas such as *The Marriage of Figaro*, *Così fan tutte* and *The Magic Flute*, twenty-one concertos, symphonies, string quartets, serenades and masses.

Paderewski, Ignace (1860–1941) Polish pianist, composer and statesman. He raised money for Poland during World War I by giving piano concerts, interpreting works by Chopin, Liszt and Schumann in particular. He became Prime Minister of Poland in 1919. He composed an opera, a piano concerto, numerous works for solo piano and a symphony in the Romantic style.

Paganini, Niccolo (1782–1840) Italian composer and violinist famed for his extraordinary virtuosity. His compositions, mainly for the violin, include four violin concertos and numerous variations and 'Capricci' for unaccompanied violin. Some of his works were later transcribed for piano by Schumann, among others.

Prokofiev, Sergei (1891–1953) Russian composer and pianist. Left Russia in 1918; established himself as a composer and performer in Europe and America before returning to Russia in 1934. His works after this date became slightly less original. Wrote several ballets, 'Romeo and Juliet' and 'Cinderella' among them, a number of operas, seven symphonies, five piano concertos, two violin concertos, piano sonatas and songs.

Puccini, Giacomo (1858–1924) Italian composer, almost entirely of operatic works; these include *Tosca*, *La Bohème*, *Turandot* and *Madame Butterfly*.

Rachmaninov, Sergei (1873–1943) Russian composer and pianist who took up permanent residence in America in 1918; his music was banned in Russia for a long period. He toured as a conductor and pianist and his most famous works are those for the piano – his four piano concertos, two-piano works and piano solos.

Ravel, Maurice (1875–1937) French composer; like Debussy an Impressionist. Considered an innovator in piano technique, he composed many works for this instrument as well as an opera, a ballet and a number of orchestral pieces.

Reizenstein, Franz (1911–1968) German-born composer who lived in England from 1934 and was a pupil of Vaughan Williams. His works include a cello concerto and sonatas, piano concertos and many pieces for solo piano, a cantata and the radio opera *Anna Kraus*.

Rimsky-Korsakov, Nikolai (1844–1908) Russian nationalist and dramatic composer. Wrote fifteen operas, including *Ivan the Terrible* and *The Golden Cockerel* – banned in Russia after his death – three symphonies, the symphonic suite 'Scheherazade', a piano concerto and various folk song arrangements.

Rossini, Gioacchino (1792–1868) Italian composer, mainly of opera, and director of the San Carlo opera in Naples and the Théâtre Italien, Paris. Between the ages of eighteen and thirty-seven he wrote nearly forty operas, including *The Barber of Seville*, *Tancredi*, *Cenerentola* and *Otello*; *William Tell* (1829) was his last. His other works consist of some church music, a few songs and duets, and piano pieces.

Schoenberg, Arnold (1874–1951) Austrian-born composer, he settled in America in 1933. He developed a technique of composition which ignored keys (atonality) and this he formalized into the twelve-tone technique, which was of considerable influence among contemporary composers. His works include 'Pierre', 'Lunaire', 'A Cycle of Twenty-One Poems', the opera *Moses and Aaron*, the symphonic poem 'Pelléas and Mélisande', a piano concerto, a violin concerto and two chamber symphonies.

Schubert, Franz Peter (1797–1828) Austrian composer. Although he wrote symphonies, sonatas and string quartets he is most famous for his songs, of which there are about six hundred; he is considered the master of this form.

Schumann, Robert (1810–1856) German Romantic composer, particularly known for his piano music and songs; he also wrote chamber music, four symphonies and a piano concerto. His wife Clara, the daughter of his piano teacher Wieck, was herself renowned for her interpretation of his piano works and those of Chopin.

Sessions, Roger (b. 1896) American composer and music teacher. His compositions include eight symphonies, a violin concerto, an opera, *The Trial of Lucullus*, a cantata, and two piano sonatas

Shostakovich, Dmitri (1906–1975) Russian composer. His work, although condemned by the Russian authorities as ideologically unsound, includes several symphonies reflecting political or patriotic themes, such as the 'October', the 'May Day' and the 'Leningrad', as well as operas, ballets, songs and film music.

Sibelius, Jean (1865–1957) Finnish composer. His work is strongly nationalistic, much of it relating to the Finnish mythical poem *The Kalevala*, for example the symphonic poems 'Swan of Tuonela' and 'Lemminkaïnen's Homecoming'. He also wrote seven symphonies, a violin concerto and many songs.

Stainer, Sir John (1840–1901) English composer and organist, succeeded Goss at St Paul's Cathedral. His work, mainly ecclesiastical, includes oratorios, cantatas, anthems and hymn tunes.

Stanford, Sir Charles Villiers (1852–1924) Irish composer, conductor, organist, teacher and author. His Service in B Flat greatly influenced Anglican church music writing; he also composed five orchestral 'Irish Rhapsodies', operas, cantatas, song cycles and organ pieces. In addition he conducted the Bach and Leeds Festival

choirs and taught at the Royal College of Music and at Cambridge.

Strauss II, Johann (1825–1899) Austrian composer, son of the less famous Johann **Strauss I** (1804–1849). Both composed dance tunes, waltzes, polkas, galops, quadrilles and marches. Strauss the younger is most famous for his 'Blue Danube', his 'Tales from the Vienna Woods' and his opera *Die Fledermaus* ('The Bat').

Strauss, Richard (1864–1949) German composer, no relation to the waltz Strausses. He developed the symphonic poem form, introduced by Liszt, in such works as 'Macbeth' and 'Ein Heldenleben'. Apart from his operas, which include *Der Rosenkavalier* and *Ariadne auf Naxos*, he also wrote a ballet, chamber music and choral works.

Stravinsky, Igor (1882–1971) Russian-born composer who later became first a French and than a U.S. citizen. Studied under Rimsky-Korsakov. First achieved recognition with such ballets as 'The Firebird', 'Petrushka' and 'The Rite of Spring', written for Diaghilev's Ballet Russe in Paris. Regarded as a rhythmic and harmonic innovator; he experimented with most musical forms, including opera, and his later 'neo-classical' works show the influence of the pre-Romantic composers.

Sullivan, Sir Arthur (1842–1900) English composer most famous for his collaboration with the librettist W. S. Gilbert on such comic operas as *H.M.S. Pinafore*, *Patience*, *The Pirates of Penzance* and *The Mikado*. He was also a writer of music, an organist, conductor and choirmaster.

Tchaikovsky, Petr (1840–1893) Russian composer. Abandoned a career in the civil service to write music and later became the first Russian composer to achieve popularity in Western Europe and the U.S.A. His best-known works are probably his 'Pathétique' Symphony and his ballet music, such as 'Swan Lake' and 'The Nutcracker'. He also wrote operas, including *Eugene Onegin*, three piano concertos, a violin concerto and various orchestral works.

Tovey, Sir Donald (1875–1940) English composer, pianist, conductor and writer – known particularly for his programme notes; he was also Professor of Music at Edinburgh University. He composed a piano concerto, a cello concerto and an opera.

Vaughan Williams, Ralph (1872–1958) English composer, pupil of Stanford and Ravel; influenced by his study of English folk song and Tudor music. His work includes nine symphonies, e.g. the 'Sea', the

'London' and the 'Pastoral', operas, many choral works, string quartets, a tuba concerto, songs and hymns.

Verdi, Giuseppe (1813–1901) Italian composer, mainly of operas. He was an ardent supporter of the Unification of Italy and this nationalistic theme is present in some of his early works. Among his operas are *Rigoletto*, *Il Trovatore*, *La Traviata*, *Aida*, *Otello* and *Falstaff*; his Requiem is his major non-operatic work.

Wagner, Richard (1813–1883) German Romantic composer. His most famous operas, for which he also wrote the libretti, were based on German Teutonic myth and legend, e.g. *Tannhäuser*, *Lohengrin* and *Der Ring des Nibelungen*. A political exile for many years, he was patronized by King Ludwig II of Bavaria; later he settled in Bayreuth, where he founded the Wagner Festival Theatre with the help of his wife Cosima, daughter of Liszt.

Waldteufel, Emile (1837–1915) French pianist and composer of very popular waltzes.

Wallace, William Vincent (1812–1865) Irish composer, violinist and organist. Travelled the world. Composed two operas which were great contemporary successes, *Maritana* and *Lurline*, also light piano compositions.

Walmisley, Thomas Attwood (1814–1856) English composer and organist. Appointed Professor of Music at Cambridge aged twenty-two; he wrote some of the most successful church music of his period.

Walton, Sir William (b. 1902) English composer. His early work includes 'Façade', a piece originally written to accompany a recitation of Edith Sitwell's poems and later arranged for ballet. Among his other works are the operas *The Bear* and *Troilus and Cressida*, the oratorio *Belshazzar's Feast*, viola and violin concertos and two symphonies.

Wesley, Samuel Sebastian (1810–1876) English ecclesiastical composer and organist at the cathedrals of Hereford, Exeter, Winchester and Gloucester. He was the illegitimate grandson of Charles Wesley, one of the founders of the Methodist movement.

Widor, Charles Marie (1845–1937) French composer and organist at St Sulpice, Paris; succeeded Franck as organ professor at the Paris Conservatoire. Best known for his organ compositions.

Wolf, Hugo (1860–1903) Austrian composer and music critic, an enthusiastic admirer of Wagner. Composed mainly songs, many of which were settings of German poems, including a number by Goethe, and translations of Italian and Spanish poems.

Index

Acknowledgements

The author and publishers would like to thank Group-Captain Ayr at Chequers, E. V. Quinn, Librarian at Balliol College, Oxford, Jane Rash at the London Symphony Orchestra, and the Revd. J. H. R. de Sausmarez, Rural Dean of Thanet, for their kind help with illustrations. Photographs and illustrations have been supplied by, or are reproduced by kind permission of, the following people and organizations: Archiv für Kunst und Geschichte, page 84 *top left;* Associated Press, 159 *top;* Erich Auerbach, 14, 20, 24–5, 52, 63, 65 *bottom left and right,* 76–7 *bottom,* 88 *inset,* 89 *insets,* 95 *bottom,* 133, 138, 138–9, 140, 144, 146 *top left,* 146–7 *top;* Balliol College, Oxford, 28 *bottom right,* 48, 51; Lady Barbirolli, 68–9 *top;* Bavaria Verlag, 74; Bildarchiv Preussische Kulturbesitz, 28 *top,* 32, 33, 36, 37, 86 *top left,* 86–7 (Louvre, Paris), 149; B.B.C. Omnibus documentary *The Other Heath,* produced by Ian Engleman, 40, 91; B.B.C. Photo Library, 128–9, 129 *top;* Camera Press, 96 *top,* 97 *top,* 136–7, 164–5, 171, 172, 177, 178, 190; Carnegie Hall, 68–9 *bottom;* Cooper Bridgeman Library, 82 (British Museum), 84 *top right and bottom* (Thomas Coram Foundation); *Daily Mail,* 156 (photo: Nick Rogers), 157 (photo: Nick Rogers); *Daily Telegraph,* 67; Department of the Environment, 130, 131; Deutsche Grammaphon, 135; E.M.I., 64–5 *top,* 180 (photo: Reg Wilson); Mary Gerson, 154, 155; Glyndebourne Festival Opera, 76–7 *top* (photo: Philip Ingram), 114 (photo: Guy Gravett), 115 (photo: Guy Gravett); Edward Heath's private collection, 1, 17, 22, 58, 62, 72 *left,* 75, 79, 83 *bottom,* 87 *top and bottom,* 128 *top,* 145, 163, 166, 196; Alan Holland-Avery, 162; Angelo Hornak, 26, 28 *bottom left,* 29, 30 *top right,* 90, 141; A. F. Kersting, 45; Keystone, 93, 146–7 *bottom;* Mary Lawrence, 96–7, 173; London Symphony Orchestra, 151 *bottom,* 159 *bottom,* 174; Nigel Luckhurst, 120–1 *top and bottom;* Raymond Mander and Joe Mitchenson Theatre Collection, 9, 70, 72 *right,* 123; Mansell Collection, 19, 42, 55, 56, 60–1, 66, 122; National Portrait Gallery, London, 73; David Penney, 151 *top,* 152–3; Popperfoto, 34, 38; Press Association, 126; Radio Times Hulton Picture Library, 10, 33 *inset,* 39, 41, 46, 49, 160, 167, 169, 194–5; Houston Rogers, 100, 104–5, 106–7, 108–9, 118, 119, 124, 125, 134; St. Peter's-in-Thanet parish, 13; Madron Seligman collection, 6; Snark International, 30 *top left and bottom,* 31, 83 *top* (National Gallery of Art, Washington), 85 (Bibliothek National, Vienna), 86 *bottom left;* Southern Television, 81 (photo: Tony Nutley); Sun Newspapers, 2–3; Svenska Turisttrafikförbundet, 117; Syndication International, 92; Valerie Wilmer, 71; Reg Wilson, 88, 89, 94, 95 *top,* 98, 99, 101, 102, 103, 106 *top,* 107 *top,* 110, 111, 112.